Law of Attraction
Pearls of Wisdom

*Essays about the Law of Attraction
and Deliberate Creation*

by

Jeff Street

Copyright © 2014-2019

Discover more at:

http://divine-cosmos.net

Contents

Introduction

This book contains all the essays that I've written about the Law of Attraction and Deliberate Creation between the spring of 2015 until now (the spring of 2019). The Law of Attraction is my absolute favorite topic within the genre of spiritual metaphysics. One that I dove into a deep study of not too long after my "awakening" began back in the spring of 2014.

Discovering My Creatorship

One of the strange things that started happening during the early stages of my awakening, before I figured out what the heck was going on, was a fantastic amount of synchronicities (very convenient "coincidences") and lots of "good luck."

My rational mind found it very strange because It didn't seem like it should be possible to be that lucky. It seemed like some sort of magic was going on or I was graced by the universe. Of course, when my seeking for the truth led me to stumble upon the Law of Attraction, it all clicked. For some reason, the idea resonated with me profoundly and all the synchronicities I had been experiencing seemed to be consistent with it.

This was the moment of truth, was I going to reject the idea and walk away because it didn't match anything I'd been taught by mainstream science, or would I give it a try? To me, the choice was a no-brainer. I had been experiencing all sorts of things inexplicable by traditional science so exploring an alternative explanation seemed quite reasonable to me.

And if the Law of Attraction were true — if we were creating our reality not only with our choices and actions but also with our thoughts and desires — then this would be the most empowering knowledge of anyone's existence! You'd have to be crazy not to keep an open mind, learn the principles and practices, and do some experiments. After all, you'd have so much to gain, and so very little too lose.

And as I began to learn and experiment with the Law of Attraction and Deliberate Creation, I was routinely manifesting undeniable results. And the more that I learned and practiced the more blatantly obvious it was that there was a strong correlation between my thoughts and desires and what was showing up. Oh my god! This Law of Attraction thing was real! We are creating our reality with our thoughts (and more)! I was completely ecstatic at the discovery of my creatorship!

Incredible! Our thoughts effect our reality! Perhaps this is why the Buddha said the following:

Your worst enemy cannot harm you as much as your own unguarded thoughts

---

I considered the possibility that I might be going crazy, but after discovering that many other people were practicing deliberate creation and also getting undeniable results, I decided to just accept that it was true. Woooh! I really am a creator! And so is everyone else whether they know it or not!

Needless to say, once you discover that you are creating your reality with your thoughts there's no going back. So, I dove even deeper into my study and experimentation with the principles and practices of the Law of Attraction and Deliberate Creation. I had a burning desire to become a master of manifestation!

I also had a burning desire to share this empowering knowledge, and my experiences and insights about it, with anyone with an open mind. That's why I started my website Divine Cosmos and started writing about all aspects of spiritual metaphysics including the Law of Attraction.

And that's why I've packaged everything I've written about this subject into this book. I hope you find it helpful.

Enjoy,

Jeff

Chapter 1

Discovered Your Creatorship? Manifesting 101

Did you know that through the power of your God-Self you are creating your personal reality with your thoughts and beliefs? You are a creator, and you have the potential to manifest the life of your dreams. But to fully tap into your creative potential, you'll have to fully embrace your creatorship, master the laws of creation, and overcome many mental limitations — and this is no small task.

Many wise spiritual sages throughout the ages have alluded to the fact that we are creating our reality with our thoughts. The great roman emperor and spiritual philosopher Marcus Aurelius uttered these timeless words: *"Our life is what our thoughts make it."* The Buddha uttered these words of wisdom, *"With our thoughts we make the world."* The Buddha expanded on this idea when he made the statement, *"What you think, you become. What you feel, you attract. What you imagine, you create."* Henry David Thoreau, the great American essayist, poet, and philosopher wrote these words, *"This world is but a canvas for our imagination."*

Why Isn't It Working for Me?

Actually, it IS working for you, but not the way you think. You are ALWAYS creating your reality; always getting exactly what you think, expect, and believe. But if you aren't completely clear about what you desire, completely focused on it, completely positive, and completely free from limiting beliefs what you create for yourself will fall far short of your potential. Many of us are putting in plenty of effort but don't realize the many things we are doing that are counteracting much of it.

The famous Law of Attraction teacher, Esther Hicks, alluded to the fact that most of us are sabotaging the manifestation of our true desires, and pointed to the primary reason we are doing so, when she said:

> *When you no longer split your flow of energy with contradictory thoughts, you'll know your power.*

In this article, I'll introduce you to some of the more important principles, techniques, and pitfalls of manifesting. Before we get into the nitty-gritty, let's take a little side trip.

Got Happiness, Fulfillment, Success, and Abundance?

Many of us are not satisfied with our lives — we aren't happy with our jobs, where we live, or how much money we make. Many of us aren't achieving the success, abundance, and happiness we yearn for. Instead of dreaming big and following our passion we are settling for what seems practical and doable. We're afraid to take a chance and follow our passion and our dreams.

What do you DESIRE and how do you define SUCCESS? Everyone defines success differently; some of us desire fame and fortune, others want to live a life of adventure, still others want to serve humanity. Whatever you desire, it's just fine with the Universe. It gave you free will so you could explore and experience as you see fit. It does not judge you or your desires. It is OK with you creating whatever experiences you like. This does not mean it is totally indifferent about what experiences you create for yourself. The Universe is experiencing through you, so when you're happy it's happy. It wants you to BE what you desire, and to HAVE what you desire.

In fact, it's not sitting around passively watching you strive towards your aspirations and desires. If you are willing to put your full will and effort towards what you desire, it will support you; it will empower you. It is delighted when you dream big and courageously follow your passion. It will match your desire, passion, will, and effort every step of the way. If you are willing to put your heart and soul into it, the Universe will be delighted to help you.

The famous ancient Greek playwright, Aeschylus, echoed this idea when he said:

> *When a man is willing and eager, the gods join in.*

The way the Universe helps you attain your desires is by providing favorable circumstances and opportunities. It doesn't just dump a pot of gold in your lap, not in the Earth game anyway. It expects you to work hard for your desired outcomes. It expects you to demonstrate that you really want it. So, it presents opportunities and it's your responsibility to notice them and choose to act on them.

The Rules of the Game

The rules of the game that are the basis for all the manifesting skills and techniques are the *Universal Spiritual Laws*. These laws are statements of the dynamics that source consciousness (god) put in place when it created the physical reality system, we are playing in. These rules govern how the game of life works and, if fully understood, can make you a master-level player. The most well know of these laws is the *Law of Attraction*. This law states that your thoughts and intentions attract similar experiences into your reality. It is one of the key laws that apply to manifesting, but there are many and they all apply to a certain extent. These laws are the underlying reason for all the manifesting techniques. For the purposes of this article, we will focus on practical manifesting techniques and ignore their theoretical underpinnings.

Key Elements of Powerful Manifesting

Stated in its simplest form, your **thoughts, words, and deeds** create your reality. But of course, there are many details and nuances involved that aren't necessarily obvious. Here are some of them...

Strong Desire and Intent

The **strength of your desire** is where most of your manifesting power comes from. The Universe senses the strength of your desire by how strong your associated EMOTION is. Feel your desire deeply and intensely to let the Universe know you mean business. It also doesn't hurt to TELL the Universe (out load) your desires and goals. The Universe is listening to what you SAY as well as what you FEEL.

The **clarity of your desire** is also very important. You have to be very clear about what you want. If you are fuzzy about what you want, your results will be fuzzy as well.

The clarity and strength of your desire alone will only get you so far. You must commit mentally to getting the result you desire — you have to have **strong intent** to achieve your goal. Strong intent is demonstrated to the Universe in a number of ways.

One way strong intent is demonstrated is by **making plans**. When the Universe sees you making plans to reach your goals it says, "*Wow, you're serious about this, I'm going give you support.*" By the way, don't keep your goals and plans secret, TELL people. The act of telling others demonstrates commitment, and the Universe is watching. Also, writing your desires and plans down on paper is very powerful. Especially if you then tack it on your wall and read it regularly.

Another way that strong intent is demonstrated is by **taking action** in the direction of your goals on a regular basis. The classic adage applies here — *action speaks louder than words* (or thoughts). When the Universe sees you taking action to reach your goal it says, "*Wow, you're really serious about this, I'm going give you even more support. I'm going to offer up some very fortuitous opportunities for you to take advantage of.*" By the way, the actions you take don't have to be BIG and HARD. Small actions count. It's usually more effective to take many baby steps rather than trying to take steps that are too big and eventually giving up because it's too hard.

In addition, you have to **fully expect** that you can achieve your goal — you have to **believe** you can do it. It's one thing to want something, but it's quite another to believe (expect) you will have it. It is very common for people to have strong desire and intent but deep inside, without really being aware of it, they don't really believe it. YOU GET EXACTLY WHAT YOU EXPECT. So, expect the best, and that's what you'll get!

Actions

Taking actions that are congruent with your goal is vitally important to successful and powerful manifesting, but not in the way you think. Think of action as the strongest form of intention. Strong intention without supporting action is not very powerful. When the Universe sees you following through on your intention with action, it is convinced you really want to achieve your goal and starts giving you its full support. The way to tell that the Universe is fully supporting you is that many fortuitous coincidences and opportunities will appear to help you along your way. Make sure you stay alert for these and grab them when they appear.

Generally, the more action, the better, but here's the good part: small actions (baby steps) on a regular basis are very powerful. So, don't overdo it — pace yourself so you make the finish line. One of the biggest mistakes people make is over doing it, burning out, and then giving up. Slow and steady is the best approach.

Focus

If you divide your **attention**, you are diluting your power. Give the things that you want the most, the most attention — **prioritize**! Let go of things that are no longer serving your priorities. Remember the adage "What you focus on grows, what you focus on you attract" and always focus on what you want, not on what you don't.

Gratitude and Appreciation

Gratitude is one of the secret sauces of powerful manifesting. One of the best ways to boost your manifesting power is to be **thankful and appreciative** of all the opportunities and abundance that the Universe provides. Even if you don't get exactly what you envisioned, you should fully appreciate what is offered. Heartfelt appreciation amplifies your manifesting power. Acknowledge and thank the Universe for the help it has provided.

One of the most powerful ways to show gratitude is by **sharing your abundance** with others. The Universe considers sharing the highest form of gratitude! Any abundance shared will eventually be returned many times over.

Other Tools and Techniques

There are a whole bunch of tools and techniques that can enhance your manifesting power I won't get into in this article, other than naming some of them: visualization, affirmations, prayers, and decrees. More on these in future articles, follow the blog to stay tuned.

The Top 3 Reasons Your Manifesting Power is Weak

1. Limiting Beliefs

Beliefs are your assumptions about how things are or should be. They are often operating sub-consciously — you are not aware of them. Many people have counterproductive beliefs lurking in the recesses of their mind. Let's discuss the most insidious of them.

A very common problem is **lack of self-worth**. Deep down inside you may feel undeserving and unworthy of success. Despite the experiences that have led to your feelings of unworthiness, you must TRUST that you deserve good things. Let go of your perceived shortcomings, and past experiences, and focus on creating the new you. Don't be a prisoner of your past — don't define yourself by what you've done in the past — don't let it limit what you do in the NOW! REIMAGINE and RECREATE yourself!

Step into your power and live up to your potential by thinking and believing that you are worthy of success on all levels. Success, abundance, and prosperity are your divine birthright!

Related to feelings of unworthiness and undeservedness is not **believing in YOURSELF** — not believing you are capable, smart, and effective, and can achieve any goal you set your will and efforts towards. Something Confucius said seems appropriate here, "*He who says he CAN and says he CAN'T are both usually right.*"

Another very insidious limiting belief is what I'll refer to as **Money Lack Mindset**. If there's one area where people are holding onto a bunch of negative beliefs, it's in the area of money. Many of us are carrying around dis-empowering beliefs about money that are hurting our ability to make more of it. Here are some of the common beliefs about wealth and money that may be lurking in your head:

- Money doesn't grow on trees.
- It's easier for a camel to go through the eye of a needle than for someone who is rich to enter the gates of heaven.
- Rich people are selfish and greedy.
- Rich people must have taken the money others.

These beliefs are negative generalizations and in many cases are simply not true. Perhaps the best way to dissolve these negative money beliefs is to think about money as a means to do more good in the world. The more you have, the more you can share. The more you have, the more you can invest in purpose-driven enterprises to improve the world.

2. Negative Thoughts and Words

Every word you speak, write, and think must be as POSITIVE as possible and congruent with your desires and goals. Focus solely on your desired outcomes and do not dwell on your fears. Dwelling on your fears will counteract much of your other manifesting efforts. FOCUS ON WHAT YOU WANT, NOT WHAT YOU DON'T WANT.

What you SAY is a reflection of what you think. If you are saying NEGATIVE things, then you don't really expect or believe in your success. The Universe is listening so be very, very careful about what you say and think. If your thoughts and words are incongruent with your intent, you are just shooting yourself in the foot.

3. Giving Up Too Soon

The Earth game is designed to be very challenging. The Universe doesn't just drop your desire right in your lap; it provides opportunities that, if seized, will lead you to your goal. One of the over-arching lessons that the "school of life" offers us is the value of hard work and persistence. Big dreams don't manifest overnight — at least not in this physical reality system; not in the Earth game. Our BIG dreams take time and many steps to be reached — the lesson is **perseverance and determination**.

Another lesson is to have **faith and trust in yourself**. Powerful manifesting requires absolute faith. KNOW that you have all the skills, abilities, and talents to achieve whatever they set your will and effort towards. Believe in yourself and your dreams. Don't listen to the naysayers. Never doubt that you have what it takes, and you can achieve your dreams! Listen to yourself and say "YES I CAN!" And don't give up just before you prove to yourself and the Universe that YOU HAVE WHAT IT TAKES. NEVER GIVE UP!

You must also have absolute **faith in the Universe** — in its benevolence and infinite abundance. KNOW that the Universe will provide the opportunities required. But be patient because the Universe unfolds your good in divine right time. Don't give up just before the Universe gives you your big break! The **lack of faith and trust** in yourself, your creative power, and the Universe can lead to **stress and worry**. Worry is a negative energy that interferes with and diminishes the effectiveness of your manifesting efforts. Instead of worrying, just refocus completely on doing, with passion and purpose, what needs to be done. Also, continue visualizing and affirming your success. Leave the rest up to the Universe and DON'T WORRY!

4. Giving Up Before You Start

Many of us are settling for what seems practical and doable. Most of us are not dreaming big. We have tons of excuses why we can't or shouldn't pursue our passion. We give up before we even start. Don't be that guy. Get started on building your dreams right NOW! The hardest part of anything is always getting started. Dig in, work through the learning curve, and stick it out until things get easier. YOU CAN DO IT!

A common excuse people give for not taking steps towards their dreams are things like they're "TOO OLD" or it's "TOO LATE". Limiting ideas about age keeps us from pursuing our dreams. There are tons of people who have shattered the limiting ideas regarding age and success. Don't let this trap get you

Embrace Your Creatorship

You are a POWERFUL creator with the unlimited potential of the infinite Universe at your disposal. Step into your power and FEARLESSLY pursue your passions and create the life of your dreams!

To your success!

Chapter 2

The Shift and The Quickening of Manifestation

The long-heralded ascension of Humanity is upon us and nearing critical mass. We are about to experience a massive acceleration of change all around our world. The ascension process has been widely misunderstood. Ascension is fundamentally a shift of consciousness to higher frequencies and higher ways of being. One of the most noticeable features of rising levels of consciousness and frequency is the quickening of manifestation. Our thoughts, desires, and intentions are being reflected into our personal reality faster than ever. Many people are noticing this, and some are even experiencing nearly instantaneous manifestation. Depending on where you're at mentally and spiritually you'll be experiencing either increased ease and grace or increased adversity and challenges.

The Shift and the Great Transformation

It's an incredible time to be alive on the planet. The momentous shift in our consciousness is catalyzing a great transformation of ourselves and our world and a whole new paradigm will emerge over the next half century or so. We are in the very early stages of birthing this new paradigm and the next ten years or so will likely be a period of very intense and rapid change and perhaps even some turbulence but rest assured that we are birthing a better world — a world characterized by cooperation, harmony, peace, and prosperity for ALL. Just as birthing a child is a somewhat painful process, yet the result is wonderful, so too it will be as we birth the new age of Humanity.

This great shift is being orchestrated by the Universe — by Source. Our planet is being bathed in cosmic energy from the Galactic core, and this energy is raising the base frequency of everything on the planet and it is activating the love in our hearts, our connection of our higher selves, and our memory of the greater reality. The process is nudging us out of our limited and fearful mindset towards a much more loving, fearless, and empowered mindset that will birth a new Earth and a new age of Humanity.

The Quickening of Manifestation

The cosmic energy is raising the frequency of everything, including our consciousness and this is quickening the speed at which our thoughts are manifesting into reality.

What used to take hours or days to materialize now takes minutes or hours. It should be increasingly obvious to everyone that their personal reality is a reflection of their state of mind and state of being — a reflection of their beliefs, attitudes, thoughts, emotions, and more. Our reality isn't the objective external reality that it appears to be — it's more like a virtual reality, and one that mirrors your state of consciousness — it's the ultimate consciousness training system. This is the game of life, and it's by design, and our souls all signed up to play it.

Feeling Graced? or is the Shit Hitting the Fan?

It should be increasingly obvious to all that a positive, loving, accepting, allowing, forgiving, compassionate mindset leads to an experience of ease and grace where life seems to flow joyfully and effortlessly — for all. For those that stubbornly hold onto a negative, judgmental, condemning, and fearful mindset this will not be the case — they will experience increasing adversity and challenges ever more rapidly. The beauty of this is that those that hold negative thought patterns are being given a stronger and stronger impetus to try an alternative approach.

Awakening to Our Creatorship

More and more people are awakening to the truth of their higher self and the wider reality. More and more are remembering that they are part of the one infinite creator, the one being, the one self, the one consciousness that is All That Is — remembering that they are CREATORS and that their thoughts create reality (sometimes referred to a "manifestation"). Rediscovering one's creatorship is perhaps the most important aspect of anyone's awakening. What could be more profoundly empowering than remembering that you are creating your reality — that you are a creator!

So, in the spirit of discovery and empowerment I am going to share some of my manifestation experiences in the hope that it awakens others to their power. And I'm hoping that some of you might be willing to share some of your manifestation experiences as well, in the comments section at the end of this article.

Powers of Manifestation

Shortly after my awakening (back in the Spring of 2014) and very early in my spiritual and metaphysical studies, I stumbled upon the idea that the universe is conscious, and that we exist inside of what is essentially a cosmic mind. And that our consciousness is a thread of this universal consciousness, and that everything in existence is constructs of thought with the universal mind. This idea resonated deeply with me and seemed consistent with the strange "magic" I had been experiencing after my awakening.

It is a universal principle that you get more of what you think about, talk about, and feel strongly about.

— Jack Canfield, Living the Law of Attraction

So, I dove into the topic of "Manifestation" and The Law of Attraction — the idea that we are creating our reality with our thoughts. I started doing manifestation experiments and I got positive results! Since then I've been constantly experiencing small and not so small examples of manifestation. There is absolutely no doubt in my mind that there is a correlation between my thoughts, desires, and intentions and what is appearing in my life — The Law of Attraction is very real.

So, here are some personal examples of manifestation and I'm hoping that they will inspire you to either share your own manifestation experiences (hopefully here in the comments below this article) or open your mind to learning about and experimenting with the Law of Attraction and Deliberate Creation.

Reality - It's All Symbolic

When it comes to manifestation, it's easier and quicker to manifest "small" things than bigger things. Even though big things take no more energy to imagine than small things they do take longer to manifest because they will often require more than one step to reach the final outcome and therefore require more doubt free time focusing on them before they will materialize. And staying "doubt free" over an extended period of time is very hard for most of us.

The simplest test of manifestation is to concentrate on a number or word, preferably one that has some personal significance to you, and see how long it takes before that number or word appears somewhere in your reality. This was the first thing that I experimented with, and I got very excited when I saw it was working and working fast — very often the very next thing I would see. This level of manifestation happens routinely for me now.

I recently experienced three instant manifestations of word or number thoughts, back to back in a span of three or four minutes as I was driving to a friend's house. And I wasn't doing it as an intentional experiment, they were just spontaneous thoughts. This experience left me without a shadow of a doubt that my thoughts are manifesting and quickly.

Here's what happened:

So, I'm driving along, and I look at the car thermometer, and the temperature read 5 degrees. I thought about what the daily high temperature would be if it was 5 degrees now (early morning). I decided that the high would be about **15** degrees.

Just then I noticed that the truck in front of me had **#15** marked on it. Less than a minute later I'm thinking about my dad and his name "Thomas Street", and just then I pass a street sign with **Thomas St** on it! Less than a minute later I'm listening to music on my mp3 player and I decide to skip the next couple of songs and listen to one of my favorite songs named "**Hello** Again" and before I can even get a chance to advance to the song, I pass a sign with the word **HELLO** in 2 foot high letters!

You get the idea guys? And this is by no means new. I've done lots of intentional experiments like this.   And it also happens spontaneously like this frequently as well. But three in a row like that was pretty impressive.

If you are skeptical about manifestation, I don't blame you. But if your mind is a little open or if your curiosity is aroused then I recommend the book E-Squared: Do-It-Yourself Experiments That Prove Your Thoughts Create Your Reality. Check it out, keep an open mind, suspend your disbelief and give the experiments a try, you have nothing to lose and everything to gain. Imagine discovering that you are actually creating your reality with your thoughts! What could be more impowering than that.

Ok, so here is another manifestation experiment that I did.

Moose on the Loose

After experimenting with numbers and words, I decided to experiment with something a little less symbolic. I also wanted to pick something that I was unlikely ever to encounter normally, something odd, something that when it appeared, no matter how long it took, would be obvious and conclusive. I decided to imagine a "moose". I figured I was very unlikely to encounter a live moose (I don't think I've ever seen one), and it's not something you see very often in symbolic form either. You rarely see a picture of a moose or a statue of a moose. It's something fairly uncommon.

So, I intently thought about and visualized a moose for a minute or so and repeated it three times. Then I waited. How long would it take before some sort of moose would appear in my reality. It wasn't until the next morning but when I awoke, I was checking my Facebook and the first new post I looked at was from one of my best friends and it was a photo he took of a life-size bronze statue of a moose that he had encountered in his travels. I laughed out loud! I haven't seen a moose in any form for as long as I can remember so I took this as absolute positive confirmation that thoughts create reality.

Ok, here's another personal example of manifestation.

The Trust Experiment

In the fall of 2014, I moved to Montana. I found an apartment in a Duplex, but the owner/renter said that it might only be available for six months as they might sell the place. I said that was fine with me, and I took the place with a six-month lease.

The duplex was in a partially completed development filled with duplexes. I had some nice views of distant mountains because not all the lots were developed yet. There was a large field behind the development that I loved to take walks in regularly that had beautiful open views of the mountains that surrounded the area. The field was far enough away from the lights of the houses that I could see the night sky well. But all this was going to disappear because it was obvious that all the other lots and the field would soon be turned into developments and I be trapped in a grid of houses and lights with no view or open space that I cherished.

Throughout the winter, on my nightly walks thru the field near my place I spoke out loud to the Universe — prayers, affirmations, etc. For many months, I would occasionally mention that I'd have to move to the edge of town to ensure my access to open space and a CLEAR VIEW of the mountains because I knew that development would begin again in the spring, and I'd get boxed in.

In the spring, this indeed did start happening. And my lease was going to end shortly, and I hadn't heard anything from the landlord about whether they would be selling the place or not. I was a little worried because the rental market was very competitive, and it might take me more time than I had left on the lease to find another place. I thought about calling my landlord to ask her about it, but then I decided to turn the situation into another manifestation experiment. I would just wait and see what happened — I would test my trust and faith in the Universe to provide smooth sailing for me, I wouldn't start looking for an apartment, I'd just trust and wait.

It was a mere four days before my lease was to expire and I still hadn't heard from my landlord, and I was getting a bit nervous. But that evening the phone rang, and a man announced that he was an associate of my landlord, and they had found a place for me! I chuckled to myself and said, "*That's great, where's it at?*". He said it was out north of town in ranch country near the foot of the Bridger Mountains (lots of open space with a killer view of the mountains just like I wanted!). I chuckled knowingly to myself again and said "*Great! When can I check it out?*". He said how about right now and gave me the address.

So, I jumped in my car and headed over there. As I took the final turn onto the road that the place was on, I noticed that the road was named *"CLEARVIEW Road!"* I was floored because in my affirmation sessions I repeatedly said, "*I need a place with a CLEAR VIEW of the mountains.*"

When I got to the place, I found it to be a cozy country style apartment that resonated perfectly with me. I took a quick look around, chatted with the landlord, and before I left I had the keys to the place! No muss, no fuss. This is how smoothly things routinely go for me. This is why I say I feel like I'm graced.

Ok, here's yet another personal example of manifestation.

Ask and You Shall Receive

Ice climbing is an outdoor sport that I love. I've recently moved to Montana, and I haven't met many people yet, so I've been having trouble finding climbing partners. Recently I've started announcing out loud (to the universe) what days I wanted to get out and climb and then I'd just wait. Then magically within a day or less of my announcements somebody would call me and ask me to go climbing.

Choose what you think and speak about very carefully, as your words are like orders that you place with the Universe.

— Doreen Virtue, Angel Numbers 101

Here are the latest two examples of this:

On Wednesday of last week, as I was returning from a backcountry ski tour, I announced that I would go ice climbing for a half day on Friday. There was no one I could think of that was available, but I decided to trust that the Universe would provide. The next evening, while I was out on a hike, my cell phone rang and a person that I thought was out of town said, *"Hey Jeff, you want to do a half day of ice climbing with me tomorrow (Friday)"*. I chuckled and smiled knowingly and said *"Hell ya!"*

On Tuesday of this week, on the walk back to the car from an outing, I announced I would to go ice climbing on one day of the upcoming weekend. As usual, I had no idea who that would be with, there was no one available as far as I knew. Less than 30 minutes later, my cell phone beeps and I receive a text message from a friend who hasn't ice climbed before saying *"Hey Jeff, you want to take me out for a day this weekend and introduce me to ice climbing?"* Again, I chuckled and smiled knowingly to myself and said, *"Yes, I love to."*

All right, here's another personal example of manifestation.

Negative Feedback

I can't remember being angry for well over a year — this whole period of my life could be described as "happy go lucky" — super happy, positive, and friendly. Everything seems to go my way and very smoothly, nothing every goes wrong. So, when I did have something go wrong, on a couple of occasions, it caught my attention and what was very obvious was the correlation with moments of anger.

These incidents occurred a while back while I was visiting my parents for an extended stay. My mother can be very difficult to work with and in the past, I've tended to fight her and make things worse. The "new me" that has blossomed since my "awakening" was doing a pretty good job of taking a different approach and it was working — we were getting along much better than in the past.

But twice during my visit I lost my temper, and twice in short order I had something go wrong. The first time it happened, I suspected that it was an example of manifestation, of negative thoughts and feelings reflecting back into one's reality, but I wasn't sure. But when a similar thing happened a week later, I was convinced. And I was startled how fast — almost immediately. My spirit guides (we all have guides, discovered yours?) had warned me about this and these experiences were a poignant example.

Here's what happened in the second incident:

I was fixing something for my Mom. As usual, she was very demanding and finicky. I lost my temper and snarled some obscenities under my breath; I don't think she heard me. My noxious utterance lasted for all of three seconds, but it was the strongest negative emotion I've expressed in a very long time. I finished shortly after this and headed to the car to take a trip to the store. When I got to the car it had a flat tire and I was out of business.

Becoming a Master Player of The Earth Game / Game of Life

As you become aware of the wider reality and the rules of reality creation you become a conscious player in the game of life and begin playing the game at a whole new level. You begin to custom make your personal reality, and experience of life, as you desire. And you have an opportunity to become a master player and create the life of your dreams.

Even knowing the rules of the game, becoming a master is quite a challenge. It requires complete trust and faith in yourself and the Universe. It requires unwavering belief, intention, and expectation. It requires unwavering optimism and positivity. It is no less than complete mental mastery and leaves no room for doubt or fear. For those that can achieve this, they will begin to experience a life of ease and grace and abundance like never before.

Chapter 3

The Mechanics of Reality Creation

In this article, I'm once again exploring one of my favorite topics — manifestation. It's a favorite of mine for two reasons; (1) my personal experiences have convinced me that it is very real — the correlation between my thoughts and desires and what appears in my life has been undeniable, (2) The topic is so empowering and important! Realizing your creatorship can dramatically change your life and the world, what could be more important than that.

One of the most epic things about awakening to the wider reality and your wider/higher self is that you come to know that you are a creator and that you are creating every aspect of your personal reality. By embracing your creatorship and understanding the laws of creation, you open the door to freedom and limitlessness, and by stepping through this door you step into your full power.

For those that have not yet discovered their creatorship, as amazing as it sounds, you are creating your reality with your thoughts and beliefs. This is not the objective reality that, up until now, your senses have seemed to indicate and that you have assumed it was. It's more like a virtual reality — one in which your thoughts control what appears in the game, but in a very fascinating way — what appears is the reflection of your most predominant thoughts and beliefs.

> *Nothing will come into your experience unless you invite it through your thought.*
>
> — Esther Hicks, <u>The Law of Attraction</u>

You could think of it as a movie in which you are both the director and the lead actor because you are literally directing the movie of your life, whether you are aware of it or not.

How is this possible? If you've read my article *The Illusion of Space and Time* (http://divine-cosmos.net/illusion-of-time.htm) then you are already familiar with how this works and can skip ahead to <u>The Laws of Creation</u> section, otherwise I summarize it again right here — let's dive in.

Beyond Space and Time

Our true essence is as beings that exist in a realm that is beyond space and time, a realm where all exists at once. Our true selves are simply threads of universal consciousness, streams of energy and information. We exist within the great conceptual space of the cosmic mind, within an infinite matrix of information.

Space and time are constructs that provide a unique and delicious environment for us to play in. This environment provides experiences of a type unlike anything in our native realms — it provides LINEAR EXPERIENCES. Linear experience is one that gives the impression of progressing and becoming, of time passing, and of continuity and causality.

Linear continuity and causality is the perception that A leads to B, which then leads to C — that each successive state (A>B>C) was a result of the prior state (causality) and that states change smoothly and progressively (continuity). Note I said "perception" of continuity and causality — an inference that this may not be as real as we think, and indeed it isn't — it's just a very convincing illusion! This illusion of linear experience is produced by a process akin to a movie projector.

The Cosmic Movie Projector

With a film projector, a "movie" experience is produced by showing the individual frames of the film in rapid succession creating the ILLUSION of motion and time for the viewer. But of course, all the frames are absolutely STILL images, and they all exist SIMULTANEOUSLY — the projectionist can take out the film, spread it out on the floor and view all those frames at the same time.

Law of Attraction Pearls of Wisdom

The experience of our linear reality is produced in a similar manner. Our earthly consciousness, which is a thread and focal point of awareness of Universal consciousness, is viewing individual "still frames of reality" in rapid succession — BILLIONS of times per second — thus creating the illusion of our linear experience. Each of the "frames of reality" is just a static composition of information which our consciousness is "viewing".

And guess how these "frames of reality" that you are viewing are composed? Your thoughts and beliefs create and/or select portions of the information that are included in these frames! You are composing each successive frame of your reality with your own thoughts! You are creating and directing the movie of your life.

It's a game where you control what shows up on your screen and hence what you experience, and the rules of the game are the laws of conscious creation!

The Illusion of Time, Continuity, and Causality

So time, as we understand it, is just an illusion — time is NOT flowing, what is actually happening is our focal point of our consciousness is moving or stepping through the information that represents each moment of our reality! This is what produces the "impression" of time.

And believe it or not, even the continuity that we experience is actually optional. If you suddenly make a discrete shift in beliefs, you will experience a sudden discrete shift in your reality — just as a movie can suddenly shift from one scene to a totally different scene.   You are not obligated to go from one frame to another frame that is almost the same. There is nothing that is enforcing continuity except our own belief and expectation of it — we are creating all of it with our thoughts and beliefs.

And for the same reason, the past has absolutely no effect on the present — except to the extent that you believe it does. By steadfastly believing that the present is the result of the past we are perpetuating the illusion of linear causality. Cause and effect as we know it does not really exist. The TRUE CAUSE for everything that appears in your reality is your thoughts and beliefs.

Those who have enough faith in their creatorship, and mastery of the laws of creation are able to manifest abrupt discontinuities into reality. Those with this level of mastery, have historically, been few and far between. And those who have witnessed these events have commonly referred to them as MIRACLES and MAGIC.

Miracles, Magic, and Manifestation

This is what miracles and magic are — they are the manifestation of discontinuities into reality. Most people who have witnessed events like these are amazed, and most who have heard about events like these are very skeptical because things like this are not supposed to be possible. Most are completely convinced by the illusion of linear time and causality and believe that these are absolute fundamental properties of reality. But of course, as we now know they are not — they are simply beliefs and expectations that attract experiences consistent with them into reality — it's like a self-fulfilling prophecy.

If you could completely suspend your disbelief in what I have been telling you about the mechanics and laws of reality creation, if you could totally embrace your creatorship, you could manifest miracles just like one of the all-time masters did — just like Jesus did. That's why Jesus said, "*with faith you can do these things and more*". Jesus deeply understood what he was, and he completely embraced his creatorship without a shadow of a doubt and hence he could manifest miracles.

The Laws of Creation

The laws of creation are conceptually simple; your most predominate thoughts and beliefs attract similar events, circumstances, people, and things into your experience. Yet full mastery of your creatorship can be quite a challenge because there are many nuances and stumbling blocks.

Here are some of the most important.

Your **thoughts** are the primary mechanism of creation and the more focus and attention you give to those thoughts the more creative power they have. Hence the golden rule; *Give plenty of focus and attention to what you want.*

With our thoughts we make the world.

— Buddha

A major stumbling block related to this is **focusing on what you don't want** rather than what you do want. Many of us have the insidious habit of worrying about all the things that might go wrong — what you don't want — and it is killing your creative power! The universe doesn't understand the difference between "I don't want XYZ" and "I do want XYZ" — in both cases you are drawing XYZ into your experience. This is why **worrying** is such a major stumbling block and is one of the main reasons why we aren't manifesting effectively. The golden rule; *Focus on what you want, not on what you don't want!*

Another major stumbling block related to focus is our insidious habit of focusing on "what is" and "what was" — basically living in the past — rather than imagining how you want it to be. We are constantly perpetuating more of the same with this mode of thinking. This is why our reality changes very slowly if at all. The golden rule; *Pay less attention to what is, and more to imagining it the way you'd like it to be!*

Your **beliefs** are another element that is critical to the effectiveness of your manifesting. Your beliefs shape and constrain the thoughts you have and thus your beliefs shape your reality. And here's the tricky part, most of our beliefs are subconscious and significantly limiting what we consider possible and hence what we can manifest into our reality. Unconscious **limiting beliefs** are another major stumbling block that is killing your manifestation power. The golden rule; *Identify and release any beliefs that do not serve you.* And better yet, adopt new and more empowering beliefs — ones aligned with the manifestation of your desires and dreams! We'll be diving deeper into the subject of belief and its impact on your manifestations in the chapter, Your Beliefs Shape Your Reality.

The **emotion** associated with your thoughts is another important element of manifestation. The emotion expressed with your thoughts is where most of the energy and creative power of thought comes from. Invoking strong positive emotions like excitement, passion, joy, and gratitude and appreciation along with your thoughts will fully empower them.

This is why worrying about what you don't want is so unproductive — the worrisome thoughts are usually associated with fear which is a strong negative emotion which means you are powerfully attracting what you don't want! Always express strong positive emotions when thinking about what you want! And here's a tip — if what you're thinking about is invoking negative emotions then you are probably thinking about something you don't want, so stop it! We'll be diving deeper into the subject of emotions and manifestation in the chapter, Thoughts Evoking Great Emotion.

Your **words** are another important element of manifestation. The thoughts you speak out loud are announcements to the universe of your thoughts, beliefs, and expectations. Choose your words very carefully because they are like orders to the Universe. The golden rule; *Keep every word you speak as positive as possible!*

A major stumbling block related to this is talking about what you're worried about (what you don't want) and/or complaining about what you don't like — both of these habits are very disempowering, so stop it! We'll be diving deeper into this subject in the chapter, Your Words Are Like Orders Placed with The Universe.

42

Expectation is another very important element for powerful manifestation. You've got to fully expect that you will receive what you have imagined and desire. If you don't completely believe and expect it will appear then you're just shooting yourself in the foot. This is why **faith and trust** are so important and have been so widely discussed and emphasized. A major stumbling block related to this is **doubt**, which is the opposite of faith and trust, and it is one of the main reasons that most people are manifesting so ineffectively. We'll be diving deeper into the subject of expectation in the chapter, Expect The Best.

These are but a few of the most important elements of how we create our reality, there is so much more to it. Which of course, we'll be exploring throughout the rest of this book.

The Game of Life

We have all been playing a game of pretending to be a human with our blindfolds on. And now we're starting to awaken and discover that we are in a game already in progress that we can change — that we control what shows up on our screen and hence what we experience.

What a marvelous game! How could we devise a better game than this to perfect ourselves? It's like the ultimate feedback training system. And it's imminently fair — what you predominately think about you get, what you are is reflected back to you. Your reality is like a mirror — if you think about crap you get crap, if you think about wonderful things you get wonderful things. In a sense, we are getting exactly what we deserve, or at least exactly what we need to clearly see ourselves and hence have the opportunity to change ourselves if we don't like what we see. It's an imminently fair and effective training program — a very exciting and formative game. And you are a player.

Once you realize that you are a player, and you figure out what the rules of the game are you have an opportunity to start playing the game at a whole new level — you can become a master player and custom make your reality.

Why not have fun with this and see how far you can go with the highest thoughts that you can imagine! Envision the most delicious possibilities reflected in your life. Imagine and expect the very best results. Pay no attention to "what is" or "what was", just imagine it the way you want it to be. And don't forget that your passion, joy, gratitude, and appreciation add power to what you have created through your imagination and draw it into your experience even more quickly.

Play the game with wonder, joy, and abandon and become a master player! How do you know when you've attained mastery? When you are creating wonderful experiences for yourself and everyone around you on a constant basis.

Chapter 4

Focus on What You Want, Not What You Don't

This Law of Attraction Pearl of Wisdom is one of the most important rules for effective manifestation. It is deceptively simple, and most people probably think that they're already doing it reasonably well — but I'm here to tell you that nothing could be further from the truth.

Most people spend a large percentage of their time WORRYING about everything that could go wrong and anticipating the worst — both of which qualify as thinking about what you don't want! For most, this insidious habitual way of thinking is entirely unconscious, and they are completely unaware of how much they are doing it.

It's not surprising that this is the case. The rational mind believes that anticipating problems is the best approach to avoiding problems even if, in truth, most of the worrying doesn't solve anything.

The rational approach is certainly understandable for those who are unaware of the underlying laws of creation by which we construct our reality. Unfortunately, unbeknownst to most, our rational approach in these types of situations is doing the exact opposite of what we expect. The focus on the POTENTIAL problems and avoiding them are making them MORE of a potential rather than less!

Your worst enemy cannot harm you as much as your own unguarded thoughts.

— Buddha

From the rational perspective, what's going on under the covers is more like magic. We are creating the reality we perceive and experience with our thoughts, beliefs, and expectations! This is the Law of Attraction, and it states that we attract people, circumstances, and things into our life that are similar to our most predominate thoughts. Our external reality is like a mirror reflecting what we think and what we are.

What it is crucial to understand about this law is that it does not distinguish between what you want and what you don't want, it simply brings to you the essence of what you think about. The thought *"I don't want XYZ"* and *"I want XYZ"* are identical as far as the Universe is concerned. In either case, it only hears *"XYZ"* and it brings it to you. When you think about what you DON'T want you are attracting what you don't want!

One of my favorite teachers of Deliberate Creation, Esther Hicks, said it this way in her book, The Law of Attraction: The Basic Teachings.

If you focus upon what you want, you will attract what you want. If you focus upon the LACK of what you want, you will attract more of the LACK.

Overcoming the Habit of Focusing on Potential Problems

When you approach situations anticipating problems and mentally focus on how to avoid those problems, you increase the chances of those very things happening. The amount of difficulty you anticipate determines the amount of adversity you will experience along the way.

If, instead, you just assume and expect the best, and skip all the worrying, you will soon find that everything will go a lot smoother and more successfully. This shift in thinking is by no means easy for the average person, who has the deeply ingrained habit of worrying and anticipating the worst. At first, overcoming the habit and belief that you need to anticipate problems to avoid them will require lots of faith and trust, but if you stick it out you will end up having complete trust in the "expect the best" approach because you will have seen the results.

Doreen Virtue, a prolific spiritual author, hammers home the importance of faith and trust in manifesting your true desires in her book, Angel Numbers 101, when she said:

Faith, not worry, is what manifests your desires.
Trust, trust, trust.

The first step to getting yourself out of this disempowering habit is to start to try to become more aware of your thoughts and your words. It can be pretty difficult to monitor your thoughts because there are just so many of them running through your head all the time. But what you say is usually a direct reflection of your thoughts and your words are often easier to catch than your thoughts. At first, this will be hard, and you will occasionally catch yourself focusing on what you don't want. When you do, shift your thinking to focus on what you do want. With practice you'll gradually get better at this until eventually you have created a whole new habit — one of focusing only on what you want, hardly ever thinking about what you don't, and just about always expecting the best.

Overcoming the Habit of Worrying

Worry attracts problems; it's that simple. But how do you break the habit? You can tell when you are worrying because it is always associated with negative and stressful feelings. Sometimes our mind wanders into worrying about stuff without us realizing it; this is unavoidable. Fortunately, it's easy to recognize the uneasy feelings associated with worrying and these can be the cue that makes you aware of it.

What to do when you catch yourself worrying?

1. Immediately switch to focusing on positive thoughts about what you want.

2. Use positive affirmations to focus on optimistic visions of your desired outcome.

3. Ask the universe for help.

Using Positive Affirmations

Affirmations are intentions or desires that you say out loud. Use positive affirmations to focus on optimistic visions and expectations of your desired outcome. Here's an example — let's say you are an aspiring writer and author and you're getting discouraged. Maybe you are having recurring negative thoughts like *"Writing is so hard for me, I'll never be a writer."* Neutralize these negative thoughts by saying out loud, or in your head, something like, "*I can LEARN to write better. With practice I can become a good writer and a successful author.*"

Asking for Help

Whether you know it or not you've got spirit guides that would be delighted to help, all you have to do is ask. They will find ways to help you.

Becoming a Master of Deliberate Creation

We are always creating our reality with our thoughts but most of us are doing it unconsciously and our many misguided mental habits are causing us to manifest incoherently and ineffectively. By INTENTIONALLY thinking about the things you want while INTENTIONALLY NOT thinking about the things that you don't want, you pave the way for smoother sailing in your life at every level.

Trust the Universe, trust the laws of creation, and trust your creational abilities. Consistently focus on only what you want and expect the best and you will be amazed at the ease, grace, and abundance that will increasingly enter your life.

Let the magic begin!

Chapter 5

Action Speaks Louder Than Words

In this Law of Attraction Pearl of Wisdom, I'm going to explore the role that action plays in manifestation with a focus on how not only does action directly cause results but how it also serves as the strongest form of intention, which can then indirectly but powerfully attract opportunities that can facilitate your manifestations.

Making Things Happen

Certainly, in a physical reality action is an essential ingredient of manifesting what appears in your life, but it isn't the only ingredient. Your thoughts, beliefs, intentions, desires, and expectations also subtly, or not so subtly, attract much of what appears in your life. Your positive and optimistic thoughts and expectations can and do pave the way to the manifestation of your desires but that doesn't mean that action isn't also required. The big mistake that people who are unaware of the Law of Attraction make, is in thinking that action is the only way to manifest results.

When we designed our physical reality, we never intended for action to be the primary means of creating. Yet it has become that for most people because they have forgotten how reality creation works — most people think that action is the only way to get results, to make things happen. Of course, this is a natural mistake because we also intentionally designed this reality so we would forget a lot of things when we incarnate into it.

You did not intend to create through action —
you intended to use your body to enjoy that
which you created through your thought.

— Esther Hicks, The Law of Attraction

But of course, this doesn't mean action is never required to manifesting your desires — it most certainly is when applied appropriately (which I explain further later in this article), but it is not the primary means of manifesting — thoughts and intention are. But even when you understand this it's still a hard habit to break.

When deliberately creating via your thoughts, the amount of action required will generally be is less and the amount of work involved will generally be easier. Instead of always jumping into action to get the things that you want; think them, visualize them, and expect them into existence. This will attract guidance and inspiration, and you will be led to the perfect action that will take you in the direction of the manifestation of your desires.

Every manifestation starts with a wish or desire, which then leads to the setting of an intention, and then to thoughts of having the desired fulfilled. Action is the last step in the creation process.

Desire → Intention → Thoughts → Action

When you take the time to deliberately think about and expect what you desire the universe will provide the information, ideas, circumstances, people, and opportunities needed to facilitate the fulfillment of that desire and net effect will be that much less effort will be required to manifest that desire. Without paving the way with your thoughts, the amount of action and effort required is often substantially more. Don't become impatient and try to make it happen by jumping into action prematurely.

When you pre-pave, positively anticipate with your thoughts, the action required is far less, and the action is much more satisfying.

— Esther Hicks, The Law of Attraction

Even though we generally over-use action, often time some sort of action at some point will be required — you can't expect the universe to plop your wish into your lap without taking any action at all. Sometimes you can manifest small things without a single choice, decision, or action being made or taken. Thinking an open parking place into existence, or other things on that scale are examples. But most things require one or more choices and actions to get you all the way to the fulfillment of your wish. The bigger the thing generally the more action steps will be required.

As an example; you can't just sit around at home and expect to meet those new friends you've been hoping for — people are not likely to just knock on your door. You've got to get out of the house and give the universe a chance to deliver.

Action Plays Two Roles in Manifesting Your Desires

1. Initial Action

Initial Action is used early in the manifestation process to amplify the strength of your thoughts and intentions and thus your creative power to attract opportunities that facilitate the full manifestation of your desires.

In the early stages of trying to manifest your larger desires (your big dreams) taking small action steps (baby steps) in the general direction of your dream will enhance your manifestation power dramatically.

2. Inspired Action

Inspired Action is the action you take when you notice, seize, and follow through on the opportunities that you have attracted via your deliberate thought, intention, and initial actions. These inspired actions will lead you all the way to your goal if you take them. That's the key part — you've got to pay attention for and seize those opportunities. They can appear in unexpected ways and forms — as information, ideas, people, circumstances, etc.

The Power of Initial Action

Just diving in and getting started is very powerful. Even if you're not sure exactly what to do just doing something, anything, that's heading in the right general direction is immensely important. Here's why...

Action Is the Strongest Form of Intention

Taking action towards your goals and desires, any action, however small, is a concrete demonstration to the universe that you are serious about the thing you want. You can think of those initial actions that you take as the strongest form of intention — and intention attracts opportunities!

Not only do your actions move you closer to the attainment of your goals by linear cause and effect they also serve to amplify the power of your intention and hence will powerfully attract the information, ideas, people, and circumstances needed to facilitate the achievement of your goal.

This is why just getting started is so powerful. Taking any action at all in the general direction of your goal, even if you are unsure of what to do will bring you guidance and support to facilitate the manifestation of your goal.

The universe rewards action. — Anonymous

Action Keeps You Focused on What You Want

Another reason why action amplifies your manifestation power to attract guidance and opportunities is that it keeps your thoughts focused on your goal. Which of course, is exactly how the Law of Attraction works — your most predominant thoughts are your point of attraction.

This is one reason why the advice below is so powerful and will lead you all the way to your ultimate goal.

Take small actions (baby steps) on a regular basis.

ACTION is the Ignition Switch of Manifestation

All your positive thoughts and words and envisioning begin to attract opportunities and guidance (in the form of information, ideas, people, and circumstances) that will facilitate the manifestation of your desire. But when you make your first concrete decision and take your first action, it will accelerate the flow of opportunities. And every time you take another action congruent with your goal (even if it is a baby step) it amplifies your point of attraction.

*Once you make a decision, the Universe conspires
to make it happen.*

— Ralph Waldo Emerson

Action is like the ignition switch of manifestation. Your
optimistic thoughts and expectations pave the way and taking
action accelerates you down that road towards fulfillment of
your desire. Taking action not only produces immediate results
but also unleashes more fortuitous and facilitating
opportunities! But you have to pay attention, so you don't miss
them!

I highly recommend you read Manifestation Story #2 (on my
website) because it contains a great example of how taking
decisive action can trigger the manifestation of critical
opportunities that can lead to the fulfillment of a desire.

The Power of Inspired Action

Taking action in response to the guidance and opportunities you
are manifesting is called **inspired action** and this type of action
is guaranteed to be productive. This is not the case for a lot of
the action that your analytic/rational mind conceives of. Your
analytical mind thinks it knows best how to make things happen,
but this is very often not the case with action conceived by the

analytical mind — action which I refer to as **forced action** because it isn't guided by synchronicity and your intuition, and hence is often ineffective or counter-productive.

How can you tell the difference between these two types of action? Inspired action feels exciting and natural, forced action often feels difficult and contrived. Forced action might eventually get you there, but inspired action is much more effective.

Following the Guidance and Seizing the Opportunities

You've got to keep an open mind about HOW opportunities and guidance are delivered, and in what form, because it often comes in unexpected ways. It might come as a brilliant idea that pops into your head, or maybe as some useful information you stumble across, or perhaps as a person who shows up that can help you, or it might be a fortuitous circumstance — it could be anything, just stay alert and seize these opportunities. This is inspired action, this is guided action. Don't beat your head against the wall — wait for it and then move into action!

Putting it All Together

For manifesting anything of significant size, especially your big dreams, action is a crucial ingredient that must be added to the manifestation recipe. Start the recipe with the standard ingredients of deliberate thought and intention focused on the attainment of your desire. Then add to the mix some initial actions in the direction of your dream to kick start the delivery of opportunities from the Universe. Then pay attention and seize the opportunities as they arrive, no matter what form they appear in. Stir in and repeat and watch in amazement as your dream unfolds before your eyes!

To those of you who are hesitating or putting off pursuing your big dream because you're worried that it's impractical or can't see how it's attainable — believe in yourself and your dreams! You exist in an infinite field of potential and what is possible is only limited to what you believe is possible.

We are spiritual beings filled with infinite potential — adventuring through a field of possibilities, creating our reality, and our luck.

— Mike Dooley, Infinite Possibilities

Unleash your imagination and take the leap of faith and start doing something, anything, however small, in the general direction of your dreams, and with some patience, trust, and perseverance you'll be amazed as the magic begins and leads you all the way to your dreams!

Chapter 6

Expect the Best and That's What You'll Get

To the average person, this Law of Attraction Pearl of Wisdom probably sounds ridiculous, but you're not the average person. You're a creator in training! This rule of thumb is worth repeating to yourself often because EXPECTATION is the crucial second part of the manifesting equation. No matter how strongly and clearly you DESIRE something, if you don't BELIEVE it will happen then it won't — DESIRE + EXPECTATION = RESULTS.

I'm constantly shocked by how often people doubt themselves and their dreams, anticipate problems, and expect the worst. And not just with the big things they're hoping to achieve, but with all the little daily things as well. To become a master of manifestation you'll need to eliminate this insidious habit and start routinely expecting the best!

Expectation Allows Your Desires to Manifest

There are two parts to deliberate creation. The first part is defining your DESIRE by focusing your thoughts and feelings clearly and strongly on what you want. This sets your intention and is the creative energy from which your desire is made manifest. The second and crucial part is holding the EXPECTATION you will receive what you desire. You must BELIEVE it will happen.

The Universe freely shares its treasures to those who will meet it halfway with unlimited thinking, great expectations, and the simplest of action.

— Mike Dooley, Infinite Possibilities

By practicing both of these parts, your desire will inevitably manifest — as long as you CONTINUE to EXPECT it will. Expectation makes or breaks your creative thoughts — you can't manifest something if you don't believe it will happen, not matter how much you think about it or imagine it!

The Delicate Balance Between Desire and Expectation

There is an extremely delicate balance between the desire to have something and the expectation of receiving it. If your desire for something is weak but you completely believe you can have it, then you will definitely have it. If your desire for something is strong but your belief that you can have it is weak — if you doubt — then it is unlikely you will have it anytime soon, if ever.

Doubt is the Anti-Thesis of Expectation

Doubt cancels the creative energy of your thoughts. You must fully expect that what you want WILL happen for it TO happen.

Doubt is one of the biggest stumbling blocks to effective manifestation. Doubt erodes the power of your creative intentions, and depending on how much doubt is creeping into your thoughts it will either slow your manifestation or kill it altogether. Rule of thumb — unwavering FAITH and OPTIMISM always yields the best results!

Alleviating Doubt

Here are some of the common reasons why doubt creeps into our thinking and some suggestions to mitigate each. Just being aware of these can greatly help you to defend against the intrusion and disempowering effects of doubt.

Believing evidence that says it won't happen

Most people pay far too much attention to present circumstances. By the Law of Attraction, this attention only serves to perpetuate more of the same. If you deeply understand the mechanics of reality creation and the illusion of linear causality you KNOW that your future experiences are drawn to you by your present THOUGHTS and BELIEFS, not by past or present CIRCUMSTANCES. Past or present circumstances

63

only affect what is possible to the extent that you believe they do. For best results know that whatever you desire is already done, even in the face of opposing evidence!

Not seeing HOW it can happen

Sometimes we get discouraged because we can't see how it's possible to get from where we are now to the realization of our dreams and desires. One of the golden rules of manifestation is not to get overly focused on "how" your desire is achieved. Your job it to concentrate on imagining your desired OUTCOME and taking baby steps in that general direction. It's the Universe's job to figure out "how" to make it happen. The Universe has a much broader view than you do and will find an optimal path to the fulfillment of your desires if you let it. This path will likely be serendipitous and lead you to the fulfillment of your dreams in unexpected ways. Don't second guess the Universe, let it figure out the "how" and trust that it will guide you by providing opportunities, synchronicities, and inspiration as needed.

If you insist on HOW it's supposed to happen, you are restricting the Universe's options on how it can deliver your results and you may end up tying its hands. You may also end up ignoring opportunities because they don't match your IDEA of how your desire was supposed to happen. Don't worry about the HOW, just focus on the WHAT, and stay open to the opportunities and inspiration as they arrive.

Getting discouraged by it taking longer than expected

Sometimes our manifestations take some time to appear fully — accept this and be patient. Trust that the Universe is working behind the scenes to make them happen and don't get discouraged if they do not appear as quickly as you would like. The worst thing you can do is start doubting that it will happen, this will only slow down or stop your manifestations. And worse, is to let yourself get so discouraged that you give up — this only GUARANTEES your desire will not manifest! The best course of action is always to redouble your imagineering efforts, keep busy, and KEEP THE FAITH!

Feeling unworthy or undeserved

Many of us have hidden feelings of unworthiness or undeservedness. The idea that we must EARN our deservedness is a deeply entrenched limiting belief of the human experience. Know that you are unconditionally worthy to be, do, or have whatever you desire — it is your divine birthright. There is nothing you have to do to EARN your right to have anything that you desire. You don't need to put any preconditions on the fulfillment of your dreams — especially ones like "*I am not worthy or don't deserve...*"

The limiting belief of worthiness and deservedness arises partly from our belief in the limitation of resources — we feel the need to justify why WE should receive something rather than others because of our concern that there is not enough for everyone. There is no need to worry about this because the universe is a field of infinite possibilities just waiting to deliver unlimited abundance to each and every one of us as soon as we believe and expect it.

Doubting your ability

A common misconception about successful people is that they have some God-given abilities the rest of us don't possess which were instrumental in their success. This is far less true than we'd like to believe. The truth is that they just wanted and believed in their dreams more than the rest of us. Just about any ability can be learned, and the Universe is ultimately the source of all knowledge and inspiration — you just have to tap into it. The way you tap into it is by believing in yourself and your dreams and taking any action, however small, in the general direction of those dreams. By doing this, you tap into the Universal flow of knowledge, inspiration, and guidance that will take you to the fulfillment of your desires if you let it. Never doubt your ability to succeed!

Believe in yourself and your dreams and don't listen to the naysayers!

— Arnold Schwarzenegger

Listening to the naysayers

One of the most powerful influences that can create self-doubt is the opinions of others. There will be plenty of people happy to tell you that your dreams and desires are unrealistic and unattainable. When they do, remind yourself that they don't understand the creative power of thought and imagination as you do. You UNDERSTAND that the Universe is a conceptual field of infinite potential and possibilities only limited by your imagination. You KNOW you can receive and experience whatever you imagine and expect. This knowing allows you to steadfastly IGNORE THE NAYSAYERS!

Expecting the Best with Every Little Thing

Expecting the best doesn't just apply to manifesting your big dreams and desires, it can — and should — be applied to all the small stuff too. Here are some examples:

Example #1

Let's say you want to plan an outdoor activity for a few days from now. Do you spend time worrying if the weather will be acceptable before, during, and after setting up the activity or do you just assume the best? Many will worry about the weather even when it really doesn't matter — when there is no other requirement than to show up the activity can be canceled easily at the last moment if conditions are unsuitable.

Example #2

Let's say you're on the way to an appointment, and you hear on the radio that there has been a big accident somewhere in town causing some serious traffic backups. Even though you're not sure exactly where the accident is, do you start thinking about and anticipating being late and all of its dire consequences? Or, do you just expect the best and assume it's not on your route or will clear up before getting there, and you'll get to your appointment on time?

Example #3

Let's say you're an employee and your boss left you a message that he wants to speak to you, but he gave no indication of what it was about. Do you start thinking about all the worst-case scenarios or do you just relax and assume the best?

Becoming an Optimist

From the above examples you probably got the point — many of us have a deeply ingrained habit of anticipating problems and expecting the worst that we're almost completely unaware of. Sadly, those who are pessimistic don't realize how counter-productive it is. As you gradually replace pessimism with consistent optimism your life will begin to go more and more smoothly and ultimately your life will flow with amazing ease and grace.

Harness the power of optimism — Expect Wonderful!

Chapter 6

Never Mind What Is, Imagine What Could Be

One of the reasons our lives and the world change so slowly, if at all, is that most of us pay far too much attention to how things currently are — to "what is" rather than to "what could be". This bias is not surprising because most of us are deeply convinced by the illusion of linear time and causality and aren't aware that our thoughts create our reality. Unfortunately, these misunderstandings about the nature of reality encourage us to pay far too much attention to present circumstances and cause us to LIMIT what we believe is possible for the future. A powerful habit that can take your manifestation ability to the next level is to do less observing and more imagining.

The Power of Transcending the Belief in Linear Causality

One of the core limiting beliefs maintaining the reality that we are currently immersed in is the idea of linear time and causality. Believe it or not, our traditional ideas of cause and effect are wrong — the true cause of everything that comes into your experience are your thoughts! If you fully understand and embrace the laws and mechanics of reality creation, then you know that the past only has a bearing on the future to the extent that you BELIEVE it does.

If we could completely and utterly let go of our belief in linear causality, then anything would be possible in the very next moment. This is the basis of how the great spiritual masters throughout the ages were able to manifest miracles and magic and with the same level of belief anyone can do the same!

The Trap of Focusing On What Is

The Law of Attraction states that the more you think about a subject, the more likely it is to manifest into your life. And since what you pay attention to you are thinking about, paying too much attention to "what is" only serves to perpetuate more of the same.

Attention to WHAT IS only creates more WHAT IS.

— Esther Hicks, The Basics of the Law of Attraction

In addition to the "more of the same" effect, giving too much attention to present circumstances can also influence our belief in what is possible for the future — typically LIMITING what we believe is possible. And since what you do not believe you cannot manifest this is very disempowering! One of the take-aways from this is that focusing on possibilities rather than limitations is a very good habit to nurture.

Even worse than giving too much credence to present circumstances is worrying about what happened in the past — to "what was". This is a bit off-topic, but I want to mention it because WORRY in all its many forms is a huge stumbling block to effective manifesting, and I'll be discussing it in future installments of this series, stay tuned.

The net effect of paying too much attention to (and giving too much credence to) present circumstances is to significantly limit what changes and improvements you can manifest into your life. It's a double-whammy disempowering habit.

Giving More Attention to What Could Be

If you want to improve your life quicker, you've got to spend less time paying attention to what is and more time imagining how you want it to be — here's a little practical advice on how to do that.

Work on becoming more aware of what you are focusing on. When you catch yourself thinking about a present or anticipated circumstance that you don't particularly feel good about, or isn't pleasing to you, that's a dead giveaway that you are thinking about something that you don't want, and it's your cue to switch immediately to imagining it the way you want it to be. You've got to stop focusing on what you don't want and start focusing on what you do want. And in this case, I'm suggesting that you let yourself daydream! If your mind is busy daydreaming about something you'd like to have or to happen it can't be worrying about other stuff.

Yes, I know that you might feel silly or even uncomfortable unleashing your imagination and using daydreaming as a tool. Sadly, adults in our society are taught to be very rational and serious, which is really hampering their creative freedom and power. If you want to become a powerful creator, then you are going to have to become more uninhibited with your imagination! Perhaps the following realization might help — since daydreaming and imagining are largely happening in the privacy of your own head, no one will notice.

Logic will get you from A to B. IMAGINATION WILL TAKE YOU EVERYWHERE

— Albert Einstein

In addition to on-the-fly "Imagineering", I highly recommend spending 5 or 10 minutes a day doing a more formal imagineering session. In these sessions, you concentrate on envisioning what you want in your life based on a very carefully crafted list of your desires.

Here's an excerpt from one of my favorite books, Oneness, that strongly echoes the point of this article:

> *The key to transcending conditions, in which you perceive the evidence of limitation, is not to dwell upon the essence of that limitation, but rather, to dwell, utterly and completely, in a perception of how you would like to have it be. Thus, regardless of the nature of the condition in question, where you to see yourself and circumstances devoid of that condition, you would have initiated the process that would lead, energetically, to that very reality.*
>
> *Where are you to instead dwell, in state of dread, upon how much you do not wish to be in certain conditions, you succeed in reinforcing the vibrational building blocks for the continuation of those circumstances. For, in stating to yourself what your physical senses have shown you to be your reality, you serve to reinforce the energetic grid that magnetizes that category of experience.*

Putting It All Together

Work on making a habit of (1) focusing on possibilities rather the limitations, (2) paying less attention to present circumstances and more to way you'd like it to be, and (3) regularly engage in

"Imagineering" sessions to envision the life of your dreams and watch the magic begin. More power to you!

Chapter 8

Notice and Appreciate Every Little Good Thing

This Law of Attraction Pearl of Wisdom is one of the secret sauces that keep the gates of abundance open. One of the best ways to attract more of what you like into your life is to express GRATITUDE for the good things you already have.

Sadly, the power of GRATITUDE is widely underappreciated in our hectic modern world. Many of us are so busy and wrapped up in our frantic day-to-day lives that we don't notice all of the many "little" good things that are part of our lives.

Worse yet, many of us are so caught up in our societies materialistic mentality that we only measure GOOD with how much MONEY and shiny new THINGS we can collect. Our fixation on money and stuff often blinds us to what's truly important, and we often fall into the trap of focusing more on what we DON'T HAVE rather than what we do — a major manifestation pitfall called "lack mindset."

Not only does nurturing a habit of noticing and appreciating all the blessings in your life keep you in a healthy present moment focus but it also attracts more blessings. How's that you ask?

Does the Universe reward gratitude because it likes to be appreciated? Or because gratitude is inherently good? Well perhaps, but certainly the Law of Attraction is at work here.

Why Appreciation and Gratitude Work

Regularly expressing gratitude is a powerful tool for attracting abundance because it represents giving significant thought, attention, and positive emotion (appreciation is a strong positive emotion) to what you like. This is how the Law of Attraction works — the more thought and emotion you give to a subject the more likely it is that it will appear in your life.

Another reason gratitude attracts abundance is because it represents an acknowledgment of "I have" rather than "I don't have" — **abundance mindset** rather than **lack mindset**. By the Law of Attraction thoughts of abundance attract abundance but thoughts of lack attract lack!

Sadly, the default habit of many is focusing on what they lack, and this is a major manifesting pitfall — thinking more about NOT HAVING something rather than just imagining having it — and it only serves to attract more lack into your life!

The attitude of gratitude attracts more positive things into your life.

Slow down and notice all the wonderful little things in your life. Express gratitude and appreciation for everything you like in your life, no matter how mundane or unimportant it may seem. Appreciate the small stuff — the beautiful sunny days that you love so much, or how smoothly and quickly your commute to work went, the friendly and helpful attendant at your local store, etcetera. Doing this will give you a greater sense of satisfaction with life, and it will start attracting more of what you like.

Start noticing all the stuff around you that you like even if it's not yours — the nice car someone else has, or a beautiful home you admire, a beautiful neighborhood, whatever. This practice strengthens your abundance mindset and builds a habit of noticing what you like, and both of these will increase the likelihood of attracting those very things to you.

Sharing and Generosity - The Highest Form of Gratitude

One of the most powerful ways to show gratitude to the Universe for all the good it has provided you is to SHARE your abundance with others. Sharing sends a very strong message to the Universe — it says that you are confident that there is plenty and have no doubt that you can receive more whenever it is needed.

Sharing is the antithesis of **lack mindset**. By sharing freely, you are demonstrating a powerful "abundance mindset". Hence, it is very likely that any abundance you share will eventually be returned to you many times over.

Not freely giving to others blocks the flow of universal abundance because abundance flows in circles — the circle of giving and receiving, as per the *Universal Spiritual Law of Giving and Receiving*.

Unblock your flow of abundance through giving on all levels — physical, emotional, and spiritual. But give from the heart unconditionally, giving with an ulterior motive nullifies most of its power. Any giving no matter how small is rewarded by the Universe.

Completely let go of the belief that when you give, this means less for you. This is a fear of people that haven't discovered and embraced their creatorship and don't understand that the universe is a field of infinite potential; hence the source of infinite abundance.

Putting It All Together

Make a habit of noticing what you like (instead of what you don't like), expressing your appreciation for what you have (instead of focusing on what you lack), and sharing freely, and watch the magic begin!

Chapter 9

Thoughts Evoking Great Emotion Manifest Quickly

The Law of Attraction states that the essence of your most predominant thoughts are what will appear, sooner or later, in your life as people, events, circumstances, and things. But thoughts alone have minimal creative power. The feelings and emotion associated with your thoughts are what give them most of their creative power.

You can think of thought as the template that defines a manifestation/materialization and emotion as the power behind the thought. The stronger the feelings and emotion associated with a thought the faster and better it will manifest into your reality!

Thoughts and emotion are energy, as is everything — that's why thoughts can become things — because THINGS are simply patterns of energy. Subjectively, a thought associated with emotion FEELS STRONGER and, in fact, the energy field created by highly emotive thoughts is indeed stronger.

If you're skeptical about this, then you should try the experiment that physically demonstrates this from the book E-Squared: Do-It-Yourself Experiments That Prove Your Thoughts

Create Your Reality, there's an experiment in there that uses wire coat hangers and drinking straws that lets you physically see the effect of your emotive thoughts (see video below). This experiment is one of nine interesting and compelling experiments found in this highly recommended book which explains why thoughts are creative in a very entertaining style and from a very refreshing scientific perspective.

There are two parts to deliberate creation — desire and expectation. The dictionary defines DESIRE as a strong feeling of wanting to have something or wishing for something to happen. In terms of manifestation, desire is the focusing of your thoughts and feelings clearly and strongly on what you want.

When you are deliberately thinking about what you want in your daily imagineering sessions, be sure to express your feelings and emotion as strongly as you can. Don't just visualize your desire make it multi-sensory — smell it, hear it, feel it, taste it, as well as see it. Play it out in your mind like a movie, see yourself having what you desire, and deeply feel and express the emotion, excitement, and satisfaction of its attainment. Create the INNER experience of having and being what you desire.

The importance of emotion in powerful manifestation is echoed by this statement made by Abraham via Esther Hicks in her book The Law of Attraction.

*The thoughts that you think without bringing
forth the feeling of strong emotion are not of
great magnetic power.*

Of course, the emotion you express must be genuine — you can't fool the universe. This is one of the reasons why following your passion is encouraged by so many spiritual teachers. When you pursue your dreams and do what you love you automatically have strong, genuine positive feelings which are a powerful force attracting exactly what you desire.

*The more positive your thoughts and feelings, the
faster and better manifestation occurs.*

Luckily, you normally have plenty of strong positive feelings about things that you want. The key is to let those feelings out and fully express them. This is something that many adults in our society may not be good at — deeply feeling and expressing their emotions. This is one of the reasons why you should find a private place to do your imagineering sessions — you want to be very uninhibited during these sessions. Expressing your thoughts out loud also adds power to them, all the more reason for a private place.

One place where I find complete privacy is in my car when I'm driving around. I'll often use this time to do affirmations, visualizations, prayers, etc. and passionately talk to myself and the Universe about my hopes, dreams, and desires.

I also use my late-night walks under the stars on the country road and in the field near my home for the same purpose. Find something that works for you.

The Pitfall of Fear, Worry, and Negative Emotion

The great pitfall of the power of emotions is that if you let your mind wander to thoughts associated with strong negative emotions — fear, worry, etc. — then you are powerfully attracting the very things that you are worried about. Which by definition is stuff you DON'T WANT in your life. This is why FEAR and WORRY are the greatest impediments to the manifestation your true desires!

This point is echoed in the following statement made by the great ancient Chinese philosopher, Lao Tzu.

Be careful what you water your dreams with.
Water them with worry and fear and weeds will
choke the life from your dream.

The silver lining to this is that negative emotions are an obvious indicator that you are thinking about something you don't want and thus serve as a tool to redirect your thoughts. At any time during the day, as your mind wanders from thought to thought, if you find yourself feeling uneasy, uncomfortable, fearful, or worried it is a clear sign that you are thinking about something you DON'T WANT.

Your negative emotions are like a big red flag being waved in your face telling you to immediately switch to thinking about what you DO WANT rather than what you don't. When you are thinking about something you want, it will make you feel good, not bad — remember this.

As an example, let's say you start thinking about something going wrong with a project you are working on. When you catch yourself doing this, simply stop imagining the worst and switch immediately to imagining the best possible outcome. Imagine this outcome in vivid detail, feeling the excitement and satisfaction of it. If you can't muster enough positivity to do this, then try replacing your worries with positive affirmations or prayers for help.

Positive affirmations are essentially statements to yourself and the Universe in the vein of *"Yes It Will"* instead of *"No It Won't"* or *"Yes I Can"* instead of *"No I Can't."* Switching to positive affirmations distracts you from your worries for long enough for them to pass and focuses your thoughts and words on the positive outcomes which you desire. If you want to learn more about the power of affirmations, and how to most effectively use them, I recommend the book The Power of Affirmations & The Secret to Their Success.

If you are feeling so discouraged that you can't bring yourself to make positive affirmational statements, then prayers for help are often a great approach to take. Just ask the Universe, your spirit guides, or whatever/whoever you identify with out there for help staying optimistic. Doing so distracts you from continued worrying and, believe it or not, help will come — you've got spirit guides whether you know it or not, and they are just waiting for you to ask for help.

Putting It All Together

Through the enormous power of your emotions you've been unwittingly making or breaking the manifestation of your true desires. By deliberately thinking about what you want with strong positive emotion and deliberately avoiding thinking about anything that evokes negative emotion you can take your manifesting to a whole new level.

Chapter 10

Your Words Are Orders to the Universe

Most people have no idea of the power of their spoken words. Your words are magnetic affirmations that draw to you the very things you talk about. This is because the words you speak are simply a mirror of your thoughts and beliefs, and these are what define your point of attraction. Much like how emotion increases the creative power of your thoughts so does saying them out loud. What you speak reinforces, and therefore amplifies, the underlying thought and accelerates its manifestation

Your words will not cause instant manifestations of what you talk about, but the more often you say them, the more well-defined and less contradicted your thoughts and ideas become, and the sooner they will be manifested.

This idea is echoed in the following statement made by Mike Dooley in his highly recommended book Infinite Possibilities.

*Your words are simply your thoughts out loud,
making them the ones that will become things
the soonest.*

Emotion is part of the reason words are so powerful — the thoughts we choose to say out loud are often the ones we feel most strongly about making them very powerful attractors.

Hence, one of the golden rules of deliberate creation is...

*Ensure that every word you speak, write, or think
is as positive as possible for best results.*

Many people don't follow this rule very well at all. Many have fallen into the trap of habitual negative and pessimistic thinking. They have developed a deeply ingrained habit of focusing on what they don't want or don't like, rather than focusing on what they want. They focus on what could go wrong rather than expecting the best, and they focus on limitations rather than possibilities.

Law of Attraction Pearls of Wisdom

Pitfall - Talking About What You Don't Like, Don't Want, or Fear

Those with a negative/pessimistic mindset, are very easy to spot — all you have to do is listen to what they talk about. If you do, you'll hear them doing a lot of complaining — talking about what they don't like and don't want. You'll hear them talk a lot about their fears and what they don't want to happen. You'll hear them talk a lot about what might go wrong. All very disempowering if you understand the laws of creation. Sadly, these people are hugely miscreating, and they don't even know it.

Complaining is one of the most obvious forms of miscreative speaking. It is the habit of talking about your problems and what you don't like or don't want. Complaining is similar to worrying in that you're focusing on what you don't want rather than what you do, which, of course, by the Law of Attraction, only serves to maintain, or attract, more of the very things you are complaining about.

This sentiment is echoed in the following statement made by Rita Schiano, a successful motivational and inspirational speaker.

89

Talking about our problems and fears is our greatest addiction. Break the habit. Talk about your dreams and joys.

What to do when you catch yourself complaining? Immediately pause, remind yourself how miscreative this habit is, and then say something positive instead. Say something about what you like or want, or express gratitude for something you already have — say anything positive! Keep doing this every time you catch yourself complaining, and soon you'll find yourself complaining less and less, and building a habit of positivity instead.

Vetting Your Thoughts and Beliefs by Monitoring Your Words

The strong correlation between our thoughts and what we talk about is a good thing because it gives us an easy way to catch ourselves thinking negatively.

It is nearly impossible to monitor our thoughts because most of them arise unconsciously, and there are a whole lot of them. It's far easier to monitor what we say because we utter our thoughts out loud only occasionally. It's not that difficult to build a habit of noticing the words you are speaking and reflecting on the underlying thought and beliefs they represent.

Armed with an understanding of the elements and principles of deliberate creation, if you just start paying attention to what you are saying, anything negative or miscreative will stand out like a sore thumb. This will give you the opportunity to adjust your words and your underlying thinking, as well as potentially identify a core limiting belief that isn't serving you, allowing you to remove or replace it. To dive deeper into the extremely important topic of beliefs check Your Beliefs Shape Your Reality.

Deliberately Speaking About Your Hopes, Dreams, and Desires

The words you speak spontaneously in conversation are often spewed out nearly unconsciously, and, because of this, they certainly reflect your existing thoughts and beliefs. But you can also intentionally and deliberately speak, both during conversation with others and to yourself during private moments.

During conversations with others, deliberately share your positive expectations of situations working out in your favor, of your future, and of attaining your dreams and desires. Share them with people you know are positive and will be encouraging. If you encounter naysayers, who want to rain on your parade, just remind yourself they are unaware we are creators and we exist in a field of infinite possibilities and ignore them.

During private moments, deliberately and passionately talk to yourself and the Universe about your positive visions of yourself, your future, and the attainment of your dreams and desires. This process is called affirmations and is a great tool that can be used regularly to put your focus on your highest aspirations and expectations, thereby making them your predominant point of attraction.

Only think and speak about your desires, do not affirm your fears.

Affirmations are simply statements that you repeatedly say to yourself. By repeatedly saying what you want to experience or what you want to be, preferably as if it has already happened, you are reinforcing those thoughts and making them more powerful attractors. Speak with great conviction and passion and listen to yourself as if you were listening to a higher authority telling you about the way your life already is. Don't just use canned affirmations that others suggest. Personalize them or create your own so they have deep personal meaning to you.

Affirmations not only amplify your point of attraction, but they can also help to erode limiting beliefs, and install entirely new ones. Replacing limiting beliefs with empowering ones is essential because your beliefs shape your thoughts. Again, check out <u>Your Beliefs Shape Your Reality</u> to explore this more deeply.

A Personal Example of Using Affirmations

When I decided to start writing about spirituality and metaphysics, it seemed like a very unlikely direction for me. Being a writer and author seemed improbable because English and grammar had always been my worst subject in school. A part of me certainly held the belief that I had no talent for writing and that I'd be a crappy writer. But I had a burning passion for sharing these new ideas that my mind had just opened up to and was determined to forge ahead.

I knew I had better do affirmations to counter my belief that I couldn't/wouldn't be a good writer. Instead of starting with an affirmation like *"I am a great writer and a successful and prosperous author"*, which might have been too big of a leap in terms of believability, I decided to use the bridging technique suggested in the book <u>*The Law of Attraction: The Basics of the Teachings of Abraham*</u>.

So as a part of my regular affirmation sessions, I started by telling myself *"Writing is a learnable skill. Anyone can learn to write reasonably well, including me. Study and practice is all that are required."* As I began to feel confident that I could indeed learn to be a good writer, I then started telling myself, "*I am a great writer and a successful and prosperous author*" as well as envisioning my successful blog and books. This part of my life is still a work in progress, but it certainly seems like my affirmations and envisioning are helping because things are starting to take off in this area.

There is so much more one could say about affirmations. To dive deeper into this subject, I highly recommend the book The Power of Affirmations & The Secret to Their Success.

Putting It All Together

To maximize the power of your spoken words, and take your powers of creation to the next level, follow these four rules;

(1) Consciously ensure that every word you speak is as positive as possible.

(2) Deliberately avoid complaining about what you don't like or talking about what you don't want.

(3) Only speak about your desires, not your fears.

(4) Regularly use positive affirmations to intentionally give more attention and focus to your highest aspirations and expectations.

Chapter 11

The Ultimatum Experiment

One of my favorite Law of Attraction books is <u>E-Squared: Nine Do-It-Yourself Energy Experiments That Prove Your Thoughts Create Your Reality</u> by Pam Grout. The book starts with a great explanation of how and why manifesting works that takes a unique science-oriented approach and has a refreshingly down to earth, witty, and entertaining style. The book then backs up the theory with nine do-it-yourself experiments that will prove to you that your thoughts indeed create your reality.

Pam points out that the best way to start developing your manifesting abilities is by doing some short and simple experiments. Ones designed to be short enough that you ought to be able to suspend your disbelief for their duration (which is crucial) and see some actual results!

Given some successful experiments, it's likely you'll start taking this Law of Attraction stuff seriously and begin to embrace your creatorship — and get very excited! What could be more exciting than discovering that YOU ARE A CREATOR?

I thought it would be fun and informative to do some of these experiments and share my results as a part of my Law of Attraction Pearls of Wisdom series. I'm also hoping that this might inspire SOME OF YOU to try these experiments yourself and SHARE your results in the comments section of this post.

The Field of Infinite Possibilities

Pam describes the energetic field of the universe as a field of infinite possibilities which we can tap into with our thoughts and intentions to manifest whatever our minds can imagine. She refers to this as the field of potentiality or the FP for short. She says that the FP, like electricity, is completely predictable, dependable, and available to everyone. You just have to understand the rules of creation and trust and embrace your powers. Are you ready to dive in and test your creative power?

The Ultimatum Experiment

The first experiment that Pam offers in her book could be best described as an ULTIMATUM.   In this experiment, we'll give the FP 48 hours to deliver an unexpected gift or blessing. We won't specify anything specific; we'll just ask it to send us a gift that we wouldn't normally receive — something truly unexpected, so it's dead obvious when it arrives, and it can't be written off as coincidence.

I initiated this experiment at 7:10 pm on Thursday, September 8th, 2016 as I was hiking down a mountain. I actually made an audio recording of the request that I made to the universe. Here's the transcript of what I said...

Thu, Sep 8th, 2016 at 7:10pm

Dear Universe,

I am asking you to give me conclusive proof that I am a creator, that I create with my thoughts and desires. What I am asking you to do is to deliver to me some unexpected gift that will be blatantly obvious when it arrives. Something that wouldn't normally occur and something fairly impressive and convincing because I'm doing this as an experiment that I will publish on my blog for all to see. And I'm asking for it in the next 24 hours. I'm asking for this deadline because if we go too long, I might not be able to suspend my disbelief in this process, and doubt might creep in. And we don't want that to happen because doubt is a manifestation killer.

Thanks,

Jeff

Notice that my statement was more like a request than a demand or command. This is just my style; a full-on ultimatum would have worked just as well. The FP doesn't care exactly how you express your desire; it just responds to your thoughts and expectations.

Also, notice that I accidentally gave a deadline of 24 hours rather than 48 hours as intended. Hey, I had a brain fart, what can I say. But guess what? My gift was delivered within 24 hours! Actually, it came in well short of that, it arrived the very next morning — a mere 14 hours after initiating the experiment! Here's the email that I received that contained my unexpected gift...

From: The Editor, WakingTimes.com
Sent: Fri, Sep 9, 2016 at 9:17 AM
Subject: Can I publish your epic article "The Multidimensional Self"?

Hey Jeff,

I trust all is well. Doing great here. Wondering if I may have your permission to post your epic article on the multi-dimensional self. http://divine-cosmos.net/multidimensional-self.htm

Thanks in advance for your consideration,

Peace

Unexpected but Just What I Needed and Wanted!

This request for permission to publish my article The Multidimensional Self was truly UNEXPECTED! I hadn't submitted this or any other article to WakingTimes.com. In fact, I hadn't submitted an article or had one published by another website for quite a while. And my blogs traffic and engagement was suffering because of it.

Since my budding writing career and my blog is the centerpiece of my life right now, the growth of my blogs audience is of great importance to me. I'd actually been thinking quite a bit about my need and desire to get another guest post on another website and had been doing a lot of thinking about what sites to submit to.

So of course, I was delighted when this unexpected, but very appropriate gift arrived, and I immediately seized the opportunity. The success of this experiment is a great example of how manifesting works — it draws to you information, people, things, and CIRCUMSTANCES consistent with your strongest and most predominant thoughts and desires. Even thou I hadn't specified what I wanted the Universe still delivered exactly what had been on my mind and most important to me!

Now It's Your Turn

Can I coax some of you into trying this experiment? Suspend your disbelief for 48 hours and dive into this experiment! You've got nothing to lose and so much to gain. What could be more important than discovering that YOU ARE A CREATOR!

Chapter 12

Your Beliefs Shape Your Reality

This Law of Attraction Pearl of Wisdom explores the critical role that your beliefs play in steering your manifestations. Anything that effects your thinking effects your life. And nothing else effects your thinking more than your beliefs. The problem is that they are largely unconscious and often sabotaging your success. Here's how to master your beliefs and hence the results showing up in your life.

What Are Beliefs?

Beliefs are your thoughts about how life is, or should be, or could be, codified into rules — rules that filter and shape your thinking about what is possible. The main problem is that over time they turn into automatic rules that operate sub-consciously. Which means you become completely unaware of them, yet they still guide your thoughts and actions — much like being on auto-pilot.

The Origin of Your Beliefs

So how do we get our beliefs? Where do they come from?

Some of them you created yourself based on your experiences and observations of the world. They started out just as working assumptions about how parts of the world are, but over time they became hardened expectations which act like a lens and filter thru which you view and interpret the world. The initial experiences that birth a belief I call "seed experiences" and I'll talk more about them and their role in the self-reinforcing nature of beliefs later in this article.

Although we do create SOME of our beliefs ourselves, many we simply adopt from others or are impressed upon us, by society. We all absorb our culture's norms, but we often forget to question whether these are serving us — or limiting us. The truth is, many of the beliefs that we adopt are disempowering and counterproductive, and we don't even know it.

Vishen Lakhiani, the founder of Mindvalley and author of The Code of the Extraordinary Mind, calls these limiting beliefs "brules," which is short for "bullshit rules." In his book, Vishen explains why these "brules" are so counterproductive, and how to begin questioning the unconscious, insidious limiting beliefs you may be holding and following blindly.

How and Why Do We Adopt the Beliefs of Others?

We take on beliefs from others by imitation and conditioning. During childhood, we become indoctrinated via authority figures such as parents, teachers, priests, experts, etc. One of the psychological factors that encourages our adoption of beliefs offered by others is our deep-seated need to fit in and be accepted. Because of this, there is a very strong bias to conform to both the beliefs and behaviors of our society.

Worse yet, we often become strongly identified with, and attached to our beliefs, regardless of their source. And for better or worse, we'll even tenaciously defend them and unwittingly pass them on to others, including our children. But it is important to note, as Vishen points out in his video, that your beliefs GOVERN how you think and act, but they are NOT YOU. You can UNINSTALL them and install new ones of your choosing, and this is exactly what you need to learn how to do if you want to excel and create the life of your dreams — more on how to do this later in the article.

Once you can see the patterns, beliefs, and systems that you are operating in changing them, upgrading them, evolving them, is entirely within your control.

— Vishen Lakhiani, <u>The Code of the Extraordinary Mind</u>

Do You Know What YOUR Beliefs Are?

Want to get a feeling for what some of your beliefs are? Ask yourself some simple general questions and respond with whatever short statement comes immediately to mind.

Here are some examples from the best-selling book <u>Infinite Possibilities</u> by Mike Dooley.

1. What do you think of people in general? Are they kind, trustworthy, and good-hearted, or are they shallow, naive, and lazy?

2. What do you think of life in general? Is it easy, hard, exciting, or boring?

3. What do you think it takes to achieve success? Hard work, sacrifice, paying your dues (via schooling, apprenticeship, or whatever), or luck?

Your answers to these questions are exposing your beliefs. You might think that your answers are just objective observations of how things are, but they are much less so than you imagine. And whether you know it or not, these beliefs are having a profound effect on how you interpret and respond to the world around you, and the experiences that you create for yourself.

Ruled by Your Beliefs

Your beliefs shape and constrain your thoughts and actions. They act as a selective filter of what information you will accept or reject, and they color your perception of the information that you do receive. Your beliefs allow only certain thoughts to enter your mind, and disallow others, and since thoughts are creative, this constrains what's possible to manifest. Thoughts that fall outside of what you believe is possible will not be entertained and thus CAN NOT be manifested.

Your beliefs don't just filter your thoughts they GENERATE them as well. When your imagination kicks in, one of the things that determines what thoughts are spawned is your beliefs — they steer what you imagine for the future, and by the Law of Attraction what you imagine and think about is what you will attract into your life, for better or worse. And for the average person, who is chock full of unconscious limiting beliefs and has a relatively undisciplined mind, what they will likely imagine is THE WORST, and hence attract exactly what they don't want!

This is why it's so important to CONSCIOUSLY choose your beliefs. The golden rule for self-mastery of your beliefs — identify and release any that aren't serving you. And any belief that doesn't expect the best and give you an empowering mindset probably isn't serving you.

Here's an example of how one's beliefs can strongly steer what arrives into one's life…

I have a female friend that has come to believe men are unethical and unscrupulous when it comes to relationships — that in general, they are untrustworthy. She talks about this to me, and I suspect others, very FREQUENTLY — which is a dead giveaway of her underlying belief and that she's giving a lot of attention to this thing she doesn't like. Which is a big mistake is you understand the Law of Attraction.

How did she get such a strong negative belief about men? Apparently, she experienced a few bad relationships with men when she was young, which served as the "seed experiences" that spawned the belief. And now, with her strong belief and frequent attention to this topic, surprise surprise, she seems to experience unscrupulous men far more frequently than the average person!

Her frequent focus and strong feeling on this subject makes it one of her most predominant thoughts and therefore, by the Law of Attraction, strongly attracts it into her life. She thinks that her belief is simply a valid observation of men, yet little does she know it's attracting those same types of men and undesired relationship experiences into her life. Clearly, her belief about men is not serving her highest interests.

This example illustrates beautifully how the Law of Attraction works and how beliefs play a critical role. It also illustrates the self-reinforcing nature of beliefs that results from the Law of Attraction.

The Self-Reinforcing Nature of Beliefs

Beliefs are like self-fulfilling prophecies — "seed experiences" birth a belief, or a belief is simply indiscriminately adopted from others, and if the belief is strong enough, it begins attracting experiences consistent with it, thereby validating and strengthening the original belief, and then even more powerfully attracting more of the same.

Your beliefs may have been birthed from your experiences, but they then take on a life of their own and DEFINE and CREATE what you experience!

Because of this self-reinforcing dynamic, our beliefs can get very strong and deeply entrenched. We tend to become very convinced that our beliefs are justified, realistic, and valid. This is one of the reasons that changing our beliefs is so hard. The resistance to shifting to a new belief in the face of all the "apparent" evidence supporting an old belief is tremendous. Simply understanding this goes a long way to helping you transcend your limiting beliefs.

A radical approach that makes changing your beliefs much easier starts with embracing a profound truth about the nature of reality — there is no absolute reality, all realities are generated by your thoughts and beliefs. Therefore, any thought or belief is no more or less realistic or valid than any other! More about this later in the article.

The Importance of Mastering Your Beliefs

The importance of Beliefs in manifesting the life of your dreams cannot be understated — most people are unwittingly sabotaging their success by their limiting and disempowering beliefs. When it comes to manifesting your dreams, your beliefs either permit or deny them!

To master your thoughts and Imagination, and therefore your life and destiny, you must first master your beliefs.

— Mike Dooley, Infinite Possibilities

Steering Your Thoughts by Carefully Selecting Your Beliefs

Our minds generate a constant stream of thoughts, most of which we are barely aware of. These unconscious thoughts make up the bulk of our daily thoughts, and so, by the Law of Attraction, they are potentially a powerful, attractive force.

Clearly, we need to direct our thoughts more deliberately, but the problem is that they come thru our mind so quickly, and there are so many, that it's very difficult to monitor them. This is where the power of deliberately selecting your beliefs comes into play. By selecting beliefs that are aligned with the life of your dreams all your thoughts will automatically be ones that are consistent with creating those dreams, and the impossible task of policing your thoughts becomes unnecessary.

Because all of your beliefs are already installed, and many without any conscious participation, this leaves you in a position of needing to identify and review the beliefs, which you currently hold. Once you identify your beliefs you can then

109

decide whether they are in alignment with your dreams and desires and begin the process of ridding yourself of the ones that aren't and replacing them with beliefs deliberately selected to support the attainment of your desires.

Chapter 13

Change Your Beliefs, Reshape Your Reality

In the last chapter, Your Beliefs Shape Your Reality, I discussed how beliefs are a crucial element of manifesting the life of your dreams. In this chapter I'll dive into practical advice on how to identify and remove beliefs that aren't serving you, and how to install new ones that are aligned with the attainment of your goals and desires.

Two Approaches to Changing Your Beliefs

You can take one of two approaches to changing your beliefs. The traditional approach is that you try to identify your hidden limiting beliefs and then weed them out, replacing them with new more empowering beliefs, as you find them.

The alternate approach involves skipping the first step — rather than looking for and worrying about your hidden limiting beliefs, you just select the beliefs that you want — ones that are aligned with the attainment of your desires. And then by regularly reminding yourself of these new beliefs, and taking small actions consistent with them, you will gradually install them and override any incompatible limiting beliefs. Because of the way the Law of Attraction works, as you affirm your chosen new beliefs, both through your words and deeds, evidence will mount that supports them and facilitates their installation.

Since it doesn't hurt to get in the habit of noticing and inspecting your beliefs let's explore that first.

Identifying Your Beliefs Through Reflection

The first step in the process of ridding yourself of your limiting beliefs, by the traditional approach, is to identify them. This isn't necessarily easy because many of them are almost completely unconscious.

The key to identifying your unconscious beliefs is the understanding that they are reflected in every thought you think, every word you speak, and every action you take. If you want to discover your beliefs just pay attention to what you are thinking, saying, and doing and reflect on what they imply or say about your underlying beliefs.

Paying Attention to Your Thoughts

Because our minds generate a constant stream of thoughts, most of which we are barely aware of, it's nearly impossible to monitor your every thought. Despite this, it doesn't hurt to try to build a habit of noticing and reflecting on your thoughts because the ones you do catch will give you a window onto your beliefs. Yet, it is often easier to monitor what you SAY and the process is the same so let's explore how this works in that context.

Paying Attention to What You Say

Because we speak only a small fraction of our thoughts, it's often much easier to monitor and reflect on what you SAY. Get in the habit of paying attention to what you say and spend a little time reflecting on what it implies about your underlying beliefs.

Have you ever wanted something but then caught yourself telling your friends something contradictory? Maybe you long for a deep and meaningful relationship, but then you catch yourself saying something to the effect that relationships never last. Or maybe you're trying to lose weight, but you hear yourself complaining that it doesn't seem to matter what you eat, you still can't lose weight. These are examples of expressing your hidden underlying beliefs. When you catch yourself saying things like this you've just nailed a belief that's working against what you really want.

Here are some more examples from the book Infinite Possibilities: The Art of Living Your Dreams.

Example #1:

Have you ever heard yourself say to someone, with a tad bit of envy, "*It must be nice?*" Even though you might just be joking you're really admitting that you can't even imagine what it's like to do or have whatever it is, and your implying that you likely won't ever know. Catch yourself the next time you say something like this and ask yourself why you believe this object or experience is out of your reach. If you drill down to the bottom of this, you'll likely uncover a limiting belief.

Example #2:

Have you ever heard yourself groan when you receive an unexpected bill? Clearly you are expressing a belief that money is tight or hard to come by, and that the chances of this changing are small. Even though this belief may be an accurate reflection of present circumstances, it will only perpetuate those very circumstances. To pave the way for a different circumstance, you must think and imagine the new circumstance despite your current circumstances. That's why Never mind what is, imagine it the way you want it to be is a timeless pearl of manifesting wisdom.

Instead of focusing on the lack of funds when you react to the unexpected bill, you could say to yourself *"Good thing I'm rich!"* This has you focusing not on the lack of funds but your preferred circumstance and will energetically contribute to the manifestation of that very thing, especially if you say it over and over.

Example #3:

Have you ever noticed yourself turning off lights or turning down the thermostat at home to save money? What do you think that says about your money beliefs? Actions like this generally reflect underlying beliefs in limitation and scarcity. You might object saying that it's not a belief — that your resources really are limited. And that is indeed true RIGHT NOW. But again, if you focus on lack, by the law of attraction, you will get more of it.

Paying Attention to Your Actions

Just as your words reflect your beliefs so do your actions, so reflecting on your actions provides another window onto your beliefs. Here are some examples.

Example #1:

When your packing for a hike in the mountains do you always grab that can of bear spray and make sure you bring it with you? What belief do you think underlies that action? It's pretty obvious the underlying belief is "bears pose an imminent threat to your health and welfare". But are they? Well, maybe or maybe not, but you sure believe they are otherwise you wouldn't need to bring that bear spray, would you.

Example #2:

Are you one of those people that has stock piled food, supplies, money, and perhaps even a gun and ammo in your home? So, you can be prepared for any natural disaster or maybe even the collapse of society and social order. What belief do you think this implies? It's pretty dang obvious that it implies you BELIEVE that there is a significant chance of these calamities actually occurring and have probably spent a fair amount of time thinking about and imagining these scenarios. What are the chances of these types of events actually occurring? Hard to say, but YOU believe there is a REAL chance otherwise you wouldn't have made those preparations.

From these examples it's pretty clear how our actions reflect our underlying beliefs. And by the Law of Attraction, your beliefs, and the thoughts and actions that they spawn, are the energy that is slowly but surely increasing the chances that you will actually experience those very types of circumstances.

So simply reflecting on your actions can help you identify your beliefs. Once you expose one of your beliefs in this fashion and determine that it is counter-productive you can then start working on ridding yourself of it, which I'll dive into a little bit later in this article.

Identifying Your Beliefs Through Backtracking

Another approach to identifying your beliefs is to reflect on the undesirable experiences that you've encountered and attempting to back-track to the underlying beliefs that might have attracted them into your life. Ask yourself the following: *"What would I have had to be believing in order to attract such an experience?"* Although this approach will not always yield obvious results it certainly can't hurt to reflect on your undesirable experiences and try to understand the beliefs and thoughts that might have served to attract them. Any awareness gained can potentially help you defuse them.

Changing Your Beliefs

Whether the discovery of a hidden limiting belief prompted you to formulate a new PREFERRED belief, or you simply formulated the new belief by deducing what you'd have to believe to achieve your intended goals and desires, you are now ready to install it. Of course, installing a new belief can be challenging because old limiting beliefs are often very deeply entrenched.

Making it Easier to Change Your Beliefs

One thing that can go a long way in helping you transcend limiting beliefs is to realize that beliefs are NOT TRUTHS they are merely opinions about reality. All beliefs are equally-valid. Beliefs are neither true or false they are simply beneficial or detrimental. By releasing your attachment to the truth or falsity of your beliefs you liberate your mind to select whatever beliefs best serve you and the fulfillment of your goals and desires. Repeat the following affirmation regularly to install this new belief about beliefs.

My beliefs are neither TRUE or FALSE they are simply either beneficial or detrimental to me.

With the freedom gained from adopting this new perspective about beliefs it becomes much easier to ask yourself "*What would I rather believe?*"

Another way to make changing beliefs easier is to embrace the esoteric truth that is the foundation of the Law of Attraction — all realities are generated by beliefs (and thoughts) and therefore there is no "basic" reality that is any "more real" than any other reality.

All realities are constructs of thought. Life and existence are an empty canvas with infinite possibilities and what you fill the canvas with is a function of your thoughts, beliefs, and what you can imagine. The canvas is EMPTY because there is NO "inherent real reality" at all! There are "Infinite Possibilities" because reality can be ANYTHING you define it to be, according to your definitions, your beliefs, and your imagination!

Fully embrace this truth and you will no longer have that lingering feeling that the old belief is more "real" or valid than your new preferred belief. And therefore, you won't slip back to the old belief, because it seems more "true" or "realistic".

Installing Your New Belief

Once you choose your new belief you can do the following to install it; (1) Create and regularly say affirmational statements that reinforce the new belief, (2) Actively seek out proof of the new belief, and (3) Ask yourself what would you do now if you were committed to the new belief and start doing it!

1. Affirming the New Belief

A key part of installing a new belief is through the use of affirmations. Affirmations are simply statements that you repeatedly say to yourself. They can be used to reinforce your thoughts about what you desire thereby amplifying their attractive power. Check out Your Words Are Like Orders Placed with The Universe to dive deeper into the power of words and affirmations. In the case of affirming beliefs, you are both sending a signal to the universe and trying to program your mind with the new belief so that in the future your thoughts and actions will automatically be consistent with it.

To dive deeper into this subject, I highly recommend the book The Power of Affirmations & The Secret to Their Success.

Gradually Shifting Beliefs — Bridging from Old to New beliefs

Sometimes when trying to replace an old limiting belief with a new empowering belief the leap is just too big — you simply won't believe the new belief you are trying to adopt — especially at first when you haven't yet seen any proof that it's working. In this case gradually bridging from the old belief to the new belief, as suggested in the book The Law of Attraction: The Basics of the Teachings of Abraham is a more effective approach.

Here's an example of bridging to a new belief from the book Infinite Possibilities: The Art of Living Your Dreams.

Let's say you were thinking about how this is the beginning of the flu season and you're remembering how very sick you were in the past with the flu. Your memory of having the flu has conditioned your belief in the probability of getting the flu. Just saying "*I want to remain healthy*" is not enough to override the strength of your belief that you might get sick. In this case the following line of thought would probably be more effective.

"*This is usually the time of year that I get the flu. I don't want to get the flu this year. I hope I don't get the flu this year. It seems like everyone gets it. This may be an exaggeration. Everyone doesn't get the flu. There have been many flu Seasons when I didn't get the flu. I don't always get the flu. It's possible that this flu season could come and go without me getting sick. I like the idea of being healthy. My past flu experiences happened before I realized that I control my experience. Now that I understand the power of my own thought's things are different. It isn't necessary for me to experience the flu this year. Isn't necessary for me to experience anything that I don't want. It's possible for me to direct my thoughts towards things I do want to experience. I like the idea of attracting into my life the things that I do want to experience."*

The explicit walking through of the reasons why your old belief is not necessarily true and focusing on a new belief and the reasons why it makes sense are a very practical approach. If negative thoughts about a given subject return simply repeat the bridging thoughts and eventually the negative thoughts will disappear.

Here's a personal example of using affirmations to gradually bridge from an old belief to a new one.

When I decided to start writing about spirituality and metaphysics, it seemed like a very unlikely direction for me. Being a writer and author seemed improbable because English and grammar had been my worst subjects in school. I knew I held a belief that I couldn't be a good writer or successful author, so I decided to do affirmations to counter this belief. Instead of starting with an affirmation like *"I am a great writer and a successful and prosperous author"*, which might have been too big of a leap in terms of believability. I started by telling myself *"You don't have to be the world's greatest writer to be a successful author. Writing is a learnable skill. Anyone can learn to write reasonably well, including me. Study and practice is all that are required."* Later as my confidence increases then I'll start telling myself, *"I am a great writer and a successful and prosperous author"* as well as envisioning my successful blog and books!

2. Actively Seek Out Proof of the New Belief

Because of the self-reinforcing nature of beliefs (as discussed in the previous chapter Your Beliefs Shape Your Reality) you will begin to see evidence that the belief is working its magic. If you actively look for, notice, and remind yourself of this evidence it will accelerate the full installation of the new belief and completely dissolve any incompatible limiting beliefs that might have existed.

3. Acting In Accordance With The New Belief

As you begin to install your new belief through the use of affirmations you can also forge ahead and start acting the part. Rather than waiting till you've completely removed the limiting belief you simply "suspend your disbelief" and start "acting as if" you believed the new belief you are trying to install. Actions speak louder than words (your affirmations are words) and will spark the delivery of fortuitous opportunities from the Universe that will support the attainment of your desires, whatever they may be.

When you forge ahead like this, you will feel uncomfortable at first because you are taking actions without having completely changed your underlying limiting belief. For a while it will feel like you are faking it, and indeed you are, but, as the classic adage goes, just keep "faking it till you make it!"

To make it thru this "faking it" stage just march towards your goal intently focusing on empowering thoughts rather than doubt, "acting as if", and constantly reminding yourself that you are a creator and exist in a field of infinite possibilities and what you can create is only limited by your imagination!

"Acting as if" sends a powerful signal to the Universe that draws to you the opportunities (people, ideas, situations) that will facilitate the attainment of your dream. As this support kicks in you will find your old limiting belief will naturally dissolve as the new empowering belief is installed. One of the keys to successfully employing "fake it till you make it" is patience and persistence. It might take a little while before the support from the Universe starts to show up. You must suspend your disbelief, go through the motions, and persevere for long enough till the support kicks in and you start seeing proof of the new belief.

As a personal example, when I first conceived of the idea of writing about and sharing my spiritual and metaphysical knowledge and insights my first reaction was fear and doubt — I didn't believe I could be a writer or author. But I had a burning passion to share this knowledge so I just suspended my disbelief and started doing what any aspiring author would do — take a writing course, write regularly and put it in the public eye to get feedback, join a writer's group, etc. Now I'm getting quite a bit of very complimentary feedback about my writing, my blog is really starting to take off, and I have a book on its way!

Putting It All Together

Your beliefs are absolutely critical to manifesting your desires. Ferret out your limiting beliefs by paying attention to what you think, say, and do. When you find a limiting belief formulate a new one that is more aligned with the attainment of your dreams, goals, and desires. Then begin the process of installing it by regularly affirming it, "acting as if" you believed it, and actively seeking out evidence that it's working. As you do this your new belief will gradually install and any old incompatible beliefs will dissolve!

You can make this process easier by fully embracing two profound truths; (1) All beliefs are equally valid — beliefs are neither true nor false they are simply either helping or hindering the manifestation of your desires, and (2) there is no absolute reality, all realities are constructs.

This means that the only limit to what is possible for you to manifest is your beliefs and imagination — so choose your beliefs carefully and unleash your imagination!

Chapter 14

What You Resist Persists

The timeless axiom inspired by The Law of Attraction — What you resist persists — is worth revisiting often because it is so important. Resistance to "WHAT IS" is one of the most common traps that people fall into that is causing both; (A) present moment unhappiness, and (B) attracting more unpleasant and undesired situations, of a similar nature, into their lives in the future — essentially sabotaging themselves.

This axiom is related to one of the other key Law of Attraction Pearls of Wisdom in this book — Focus on what you want, not what you don't want. "What you resist persists" is just another way of saying "Don't focus on what you don't want." Because when you are resisting things you don't like that's EXACTLY what you are doing — FOCUSING on what you DON'T WANT! If you realized how counter-productive fighting against situations that aren't going your way is, you'd be appalled and cease the habit immediately. It might not be too much of an exaggeration to say, "**Resistance is Futile!**"

To resist something is to oppose it, or push against it, to try to force it to something other than it is. When you put your focus on fighting, or struggling against an unwanted situation in your life, be it work, debt, ill-health, something painful in your past, a difficult relationship, or whatever what you are effectively saying to the Universe is GIVE ME MORE OF THIS — because that's the way the Law of Attraction works! It always gives you more of what you focus on.

There are many unwanted situations that arise in our daily lives. Thankfully, most are minor. How we perceive and respond to these little, or not so little, undesired circumstances can make all the difference in the world in the experience we create for ourselves and others involved. Most people, to varying degrees, fight or resist circumstances like these, allowing themselves to become frustrated, annoyed, impatient, indignant, or even mad — often accompanied by complaining and blaming. And of course, this only serves to create a less wonderful and more unpleasant experience for themselves and everyone involved.

You know when you are resisting something — your mind festers on the situation or subject, and you feel frustrated, annoyed, and unhappy. And it is often accompanied by complaining and blaming, and bitching and moaning. It might be a person who is thwarting your plans, or a circumstance that is counter to your expected or desired outcome, or a policy that you think is wrong or is hindering you — you name it. There are endless variations at every level — from personal to collective, and from minor to major.

Why Is Resistance So Counter-productive?

Not only does resisting WHAT IS lead to unhappiness in the present moment but, by The Law of Attraction, it also makes it more likely that the undesired situation will continue, and similar undesirable circumstances will occur in the future! Resistance is one of the habits that is unknowingly sabotaging many people's happiness and greatly contributing to their miscreations — keeping undesirable experiences in their life.

The Law of Attraction states that what you focus on, think about, and invest emotional energy towards is what you will attract into your life. And when you are resisting something that's exactly what you are doing — intensely thinking about and focusing on, usually with strong emotions, the thing you are resisting! Which means you are very likely to get more of that very thing — which is by definition something you don't like or want!

It's OK to notice what you don't want because it provides the contrast that allows you to recognize what you do want. Notice stuff you don't want for an instant and then choose what you DO WANT and put your attention on that and only on that.

Here's a quote, from the highly recommended book The Law of Attraction: The Basics of the Teachings of Abraham, that dramatically illustrates the point made above.

Creators of WORLDS are not trying to fix problems. Creators of worlds identify what is not wanted for a split second, and then imagine and feel what is wanted for eternity.

The Power of Non-Resistance and Acceptance

One of the secrets to not attracting undesirable situations into your life and creating the smoothest, most peaceful and happy experience of life possible is the consistent application of the principle of Non-Resistance. Another term for Non-Resistance is ACCEPTANCE. Non-resistance involves the mental and emotional discipline to accept whatever arises as if you had chosen it. Instead of fighting undesirable situations that arise, accept them and work with them not against them — simply try to the make the best of them.

So here is one of my golden rules:

Whatever arises, accept it and make the best of It.

Sometimes this may mean completely letting go and just going with the flow. Other times it might mean taking a different or alternative approach to the problem but, and this is an important point, without holding any resentment. Guess what resentment is, it's a form of resistance, a form of non-acceptance, and a subtle focusing of one's energy on something you don't like and don't want — don't do it! Not only does the path of acceptance make everything go smoother and happier for everyone involved in the present moment but it makes it less likely that you will experience similar undesired situations in the future!

This doesn't mean you can never express your dissatisfaction with something you don't like — whether it's the weather that didn't cooperate with your planned outing, or the behavior of a friend or co-worker, a government or business policy, or whatever. It's OK to voice your concerns about things that aren't serving your best interests or the best interests of all. It's OK to take a stand on an issue BUT, and this is a BIG but, if ALL that you are doing is fighting against what you don't want then you are shooting yourself in the foot — you are miscreating. Because resisting what you don't like is focusing on what you don't want and that tends to sustain the very thing you consider a problem and would like to see go away.

To improve situations like these, and to make sure you don't get more like them, you must give as little energy to them as possible. To create something other than what you are fighting against or resisting you must give as little attention and energy to the problem and as much energy as you can (thoughts, emotions, imagination, intention, action and words) towards the solution or the way you would prefer things to be in the future — you must produce constructive energy.

What you focus on, you make bigger. The more energy you put into something, the more power you give it. Energy flows where attention goes, so resisting something just adds to it. It's in focusing on what you don't want that creates more of what you don't want.

Here's a pearl of wisdom to always keep in mind:

Where your energy flows your reality goes.

What if we made a habit of completely accepting whatever arises, even if it wasn't exactly what we expected or desired? What if, instead of fighting these situations, we strived to make the best of them?

I can tell you what would happen! Things would go a lot smoother, and everybody would be a lot happier! By completely accepting and making the best of every situation, no matter what it is, you'll experience increased peace of mind, and your life will flow with increased ease and grace!

Law of Attraction Pearls of Wisdom

Here's a quote from the globally respected modern spiritual teacher, Eckhart Tolle, that echoes the sentiment expressed above:

> *Whatever the present moment contains, **accept it** as if you had chosen it. Always **work with it**, against it. This will miraculously transform your whole life.*
>
> — Eckhart Tolle, The Power of Now

You are a creator, and you are creating with your thoughts and emotions. Where you put your focus and emotional energy is what you get more of in your reality. And your thoughts and emotion are energy, as well as your words and actions — so point them in a constructive direction as much as you can. Fighting what you don't want is not constructive.

This applies not only to personal situations but also the collective situations. Many concerned citizens spend most of their energy fighting against government and corporate policies that they don't like rather than investing their energy to support what they do want.

The secret of change is to focus all of your energy, not on fighting the old, but building the new.

— Socrates

The Power of Taking Responsibility for Everything You Experience

There are only two reasons why any experience comes into your life: (1) you have directly or indirectly created and attracted the experience via the Law of Attraction, regardless of whether you understand the reasons or not or (2) your higher-self designed them as a needed catalyst for your growth. This realization can dramatically change your perspective about the adverse situations that enter your life. When you fully embrace them as your creations you are then empowered to dis-create them with your knowledge of the mechanics of creation and with your mental and emotional self-mastery.

By taking full responsibility for every situation that arises and accepting it AS IS, and making the best of it, you make these moments go as smoothly as possible for everyone involved, including yourself, and you pave the way for smooth sailing in the future.

Expect wonderful!

Chapter 15

Three Reasons You're Manifesting Poorly

I thought it would be useful to do a quick review of the reasons why many of us are manifesting so ineffectively. The truth is, most of us are unwittingly sabotaging the manifestation of our true desires. And there are three major reasons for this — EG; three areas that are shaping the energy that we are putting out and hence is getting reflected back to us as the experiences and circumstances of our lives.

The Three Major Stumbling Blocks

1. Unconscious Limiting Beliefs

2. Habitual Pessimistic Thinking

3. Repressed Negative Emotions

Note that they all of these have one thing in common — they are all unconscious. This means we are not aware that they exist and hence are totally unaware of the effects they are having on what we are manifesting into our lives. Let's explore each of these in more detail.

Unconscious Limiting Beliefs

Perhaps the biggest reason many of us are not manifesting our true desires is our unconscious limiting beliefs. Our beliefs play a profoundly critical role in what we can manifest. And the sad truth is that we are largely unaware of most of our beliefs. They are essentially unconscious and acting like hidden programs running on auto-pilot that not only color our perception of what is happening in the present moment but more importantly are shaping and constraining our thoughts and expectations — both of which are intimately involved in the creation of our reality.

And you'd be surprised by how few of your beliefs you actually formulated on your own — EG; based on your own experiences, observations, and analysis. The fact is that most of our beliefs we simply adopted from our society and our parents, teachers, and other so-called authorities. And worse yet, we are at best only dimly aware of most of the beliefs that are programmed into our mind and how profoundly they shape our thoughts and expectations and hence, by the Law of Attraction, are shaping our reality.

If you want to become a master of manifestation, then you must deeply understand the critical role that beliefs play in the manifestation of your reality and you must replace old limiting beliefs with new and more empowering ones. To explore this topic in more depth, check out the chapter, Your Beliefs Shape Your Reality.

Habitual Pessimistic Thinking

Another major reason that is unwittingly causing us to sabotage the manifestation of our true desires is habitual pessimistic thinking. Most of us are almost completely unaware of how pessimistic we actually are — it's an insidious habit that we are at best dimly aware of. Someday, when you reprogram yourself to be an optimist the pervasive pessimistic mindset of many of your friends and family members will stand out like a sore thumb, and you will likely be appalled.

The famous British statesman Winston Churchill had the following to say about pessimism versus optimism.

A pessimist sees the difficulty in every opportunity; an optimist sees the opportunity in every difficulty.

Most of us are unknowingly spending an incredible amount of time worrying about what might go wrong and fearing the worst. If brought to our attention our rational minds will tenaciously defend this approach by asserting that it only makes sense to do this so as to avoid problems and stay safe. Sadly, by the Law of Attraction, this approach is actually INCREASING the chances that we will experience the very things we want to avoid.

Whether you know it or not, you are creating your reality with your thoughts, beliefs, and expectations. Once you stop anticipating problems and start expecting the best (EG; your desired outcomes) things will begin to go your way more and more often and you'll be surprised how smoothly things will begin to go.

Here's a seemingly silly affirmation that if repeated frequently will help to reprogram yourself into an optimist and attract abundance into your life.

Everything always seems to go my way —
hooray, hooray! I get everything I want and more
— galore, galore!

Repressed Negative Emotions

Another major reason that is unwittingly causing us to attract undesired adversity into our lives and to sabotage the manifestation of our true desires is repressed negative emotions. What many don't realize is that some of the negative emotions they've experienced from highly charged events in their past may still be creating problems for them in subtle and insidious ways.

Far too often many of us hold on to (EG; suppress/repress) the negative emotions from our emotionally charged life experiences — emotions like anger, frustration, resentment, fear, low self-esteem, and so many more. These emotions are negative energy that's trapped in our bodies that interferes with the proper functioning of our energy bodies which can then manifest as dysfunction, disease, and pain in the physical body. And these trapped emotions also act as a powerful force attracting adverse experiences similar to, or related to, the original experiences that created the trapped emotions in the first place — which means you will be unknowingly recreating further difficulties in your life.

So unbeknownst to most of us, much of the pain, suffering, and adversity in our lives is due to negative emotional energies that have become trapped within us. The good news is that by releasing our trapped emotions, many undesirable manifestations will often disappear from our lives. To explore this topic in more depth, check out the chapter, The Hidden Insidious Effects of Trapped Negative Emotions which goes into great depth about the cause and solution to this issue.

Conclusion

So, in conclusion, becoming keenly aware of these three major reasons that are sabotaging the manifestation of your true desires is the first step towards more effective manifesting.

More power to you!

Chapter 16

The Three Layers of Your Reality Construct

Whether you know it or not you exist within something akin to a super advanced virtual reality. One where your every thought, belief, and emotion is selecting what appears on the screen you call your reality. Understanding how your personal reality, and the collective reality you are part of, is generated has profound implications. And one of the most important of these is the complete liberation from your fears.

Before diving into how your reality is generated, and it's three layers let's do a quick review of the true nature of yourself and your reality — what you are and what you are a part of.

The Ultimate Nature of Existence

The ultimate nature of existence is that there is a singular consciousness which presides over a singular, yet multidimensional, field of energy that it can mold into any patterns it wishes by the exercise of its thoughts, intentions, and desires. And these patterns are everything seen and unseen. This consciousness has been referred to as universal consciousness, or cosmic consciousness, or source consciousness. And Source consciousness not only creates patterns of energy, but it can also perceive and experience them.

Another way to think about these energy patterns is as information. Source consciousness can create, manipulate, navigate, and perceive information in the field. This allows it to create information that represents complete experiential environments or "reality constructs" and then dive in and experience them. There is only consciousness, information, and the perception of information and this allows for the creation and experience of "realities."

The world that you think exists outside of you is essentially an illusion — it is a purely perceptual experience of consciousness. The experiences are REAL, but the props are IMAGINARY. All the information that represents your reality was imagined into existence and is essentially just imagery that your consciousness is perceiving — very much like a virtual reality. There isn't anything out there; it's just an incredibly convincing perceptual illusion.

Your reality is an illusion of consciousness — the experiences are REAL, but the props are IMAGINARY.

The way source consciousness experiences a reality construct is by creating a sub-thread of its consciousness, which has its own focal point of awareness and perception, and put's that focal point within one of these "reality constructs" and experiences it. Source consciousness is multi-threaded, and you are one of those threads — pure consciousness, non-physical and formless. And you have put your focal point of awareness and perception into this space-time reality to have this experience.

How Your Personal and Collective Reality is Generated

The way information is presented to your thread of consciousness is much like how a film projector displays the frames of a film strip. Every billionth of a second or so, a frame of information representing your reality is presented to and perceived by your consciousness (more about this in the article on my website, The Illusion of Time and Space). Unlike a film strip which has frames with content that was determined when the movie was produced, the movie that you call your reality contains some information that is pre-created and some that is created on the fly and then dynamically composed into final frames on the fly.

Conceptually, frames of reality are generated as three layers of information; foundation, background, and foreground and these then get combined into one cohesive picture. The information in each of these layers is produced in different ways and understanding how this works has great relevance to understanding and mastering the creation of your personal reality. Using the metaphor of a stage play these three layers might be considered; the stage, the setting, and the story. And make no mistake, your reality is your story, and you are the lead character as well as the director.

Surprisingly, even though it appears that you are a part of a singular collective reality with many players or actors, something a bit different from what you might have imagined is going on behind the scenes.

What's really going on is that each thread of consciousness (e.g; soul) is experiencing its own separate reality in which they are both the lead actor and director of their own stories. All the other actors in your story are just other souls playing stand-in roles in support of your story. You have agreements with many other souls to play parts in your reality — but it's your story, and they are all walk in cameo appearances.

Those souls playing roles in your story may or may not be engaged in their own version of the earthly reality. And you may or may not be reciprocating and playing roles in their realities. But there are tons of souls playing parts in each other's realities. Each soul is having its own independent experience in its own separate version of reality. How the reality of a soul, who might be playing a part in your reality, plays out will likely be different than your own.

The way a collective reality experience is generated is that the beings that share roles across the various individual realities agree to share information that represents some elements of the reality — specifically, information representing the foundation/stage layer and the background/collective layer.

The process which generates each successive reality frame perceived by your thread of consciousness seamlessly combines this shared information with the information from the foreground layer (information created, and selected, and produced by you) into a seamless whole. The details of how this works are not entirely certain, but this is how it works in general.

> *Your reality is programmable, and you are the programmer.*

Let's explore how the information that represents each of the three layers of your reality construct is produced and what degree of creative control you have over each.

The Foundation Layer – The Stage

The first layer of information that is included in the frames of reality that your consciousness is perceiving and experiencing might be appropriately called the foundation layer. This is the layer of information that represents the planet, and the elementals it's composed of, and the biosphere. It includes everything that supports human life and the human experience. This layer acts as the stage on which the human drama is played out on — both collectively and personally.

All the information (e.g; energy patterns) that makeup everything in this layer were created and are maintained by the intentions, thoughts, and imagination of non-physical beings (e.g; consciousnesses). These beings have dedicated themselves to creating and maintaining the major elements that make up our reality, and multitudes of other realities — a role often referred to as "construct holders." All the information that represents the foundation layer of our reality construct was imagined into existence by these beings! To learn more about construct holders, check out the section on 7th density beings in my article Ascending the Densities of Consciousness on my website.

The most important implication of this is that our threads of consciousness are not creating this information and so we cannot ourselves change the nature of the stage through our own conscious thoughts and intentions. You are not directly creating the stage environment, our world, with your thoughts. You don't have any direct power to alter the information that represents it; you can only choose to explore and experience different parts of it by your choices and intent. This layer is part of the information that we all agreed we'd share across all of our individual realities to create the experience of a collective reality.

The Background Layer – Collective Reality

The second layer of information that is included in the frames of reality that your consciousness is perceiving and experiencing I call the "background" layer. This layer is the collective story/drama that's playing out on the foundation layer (the stage). These are the global and collective events and circumstances. It's all the stuff that you hear about happening in the world but doesn't necessarily directly touch you. It's the state of the world, the state of human society; it's what you see recorded in the history books and discussed in newspapers and magazines. It's everything that's supposedly happening in the world, and everything that supposedly has happened in the world — most of which you never directly experienced — it appears to have happened to someone somewhere, but it didn't happen to you.

This layer of your reality construct is co-created by all the threads of consciousness (e.g; souls) participating in the collective reality construct. And we all agreed that it would be shared across all of our individual reality constructs — it is the backdrop to your personal reality — this is how collective reality experiences are constructed. The information in this layer is co-created by the collective — it is the average of all the thoughts, intentions, emotions, choices, actions, etc. of all the souls involved in the collective reality construct. If we assumed that every soul's level or frequency of consciousness was the same, then each player in the collective reality construct would be equally contributing to the co-creation of the information in this layer.

Your power to shape the collective reality, to steer the course of collective events, with your own thoughts and intentions is limited. For example, if there were five billion people on the planet then your influence would be 1/five-billionth. But of course, not everyone is at the same level or frequency of consciousness. And at each higher level of consciousness, you have an exponentially higher degree of influence in the creation of the collective reality — the higher your state of consciousness, then the greater proportion that your thoughts and intentions influence the creation of the collective reality.

And here's the great thing, even thou you can't change the collective reality you do control which parts of the collective reality that touch you — the parts that you directly experience are completely up to you! Using the stage play metaphor, the collective reality is the backdrop to your personal story/drama. Which parts of this backdrop directly touch you depends on your thoughts, beliefs, intentions, desires, choices and more. Nothing from the collective reality can touch you unless you invite them into your direct experience with your thoughts! More on this very important point in a bit.

The Foreground Layer – Your Personal Reality

The 3rd and final layer of information that is included in the frames of reality that your consciousness is perceiving and experiencing I call the "foreground" layer. The foreground is everything that you directly experience. This is your personal reality, and you are 100% responsible for creating it. Everything you directly experience is either newly created by you or invited into your reality from the collective reality by your thoughts, beliefs, desires, etc! So even though you can't single-handedly change the collective reality (because it is co-created collectively), it doesn't really matter because you control which parts of it that you draw into your personal reality and directly experience.

You are essentially immune to any danger or peril or whatever that is out there in the collective reality if you don't buy into that it can affect you. And of course, the fastest way to draw stuff from the collective reality into your personal reality is to fear and worry about how the state of the world might affect you!

Because as a creator, what you focus on you attract especially when it's combined with a strong emotion like fear. And don't kid yourself, if you are worrying about stuff that's fear.

The world's natural calamities and disasters — its tornados and hurricanes, volcanoes, floods, etc are not created by us specifically. What is created by us is the degree to which these events touch our life.

— Neale Donald Walsch, <u>Conversations with God, Book 1</u>

So, no matter what is happening in the collective reality, none of it can touch you unless you invite it. As an example, let's say that some calamity occurs in the collective reality that effects your home town. With the right "attitude" the Universe might arrange for you to be out of town when the calamity occurs. Or if you are home, you will miraculously remain unscathed or spared from the worst of it.

The right attitude to avoid directly experiencing events in the collective reality is to absolutely believe that you are creating your reality and to absolutely believe you are always safe — that nothing can harm you! If you fall into fear, worry, or doubt all bets are off!

Summing It All Up

You are creating your reality with your thoughts, beliefs, desires, and more. The backdrop to your story, the collective reality and the stage that it plays out on, are just there to create a context within which to play out your story and create your personal reality. You can create whatever you like in your life, and it is not limited to what's out there in the collective reality, but it does provide a grab bag of options to select into your life. But they are all truly optional — they can't become a part of your direct experience unless you invite them in with your thoughts. The collective reality is a distraction that lures you into focusing on what is and what was instead of what can be.

The universe is not punishing you or blessing you.
It's reflecting back to you the essence of your
thoughts, beliefs, and expectations.

Knowing this enables you to stop worrying about what you can't change and start focusing on what you can — namely where you put your focus and attention to, what beliefs you hold, what thoughts you entertain, and what you imagine and create for yourself.

By understanding how your reality is generated and that you are the one who controls the process you can experience a profound liberation from fear. And once you transcend your fears, especially if you master the other skills of deliberate creation, you will find that your life experience will begin to improve dramatically. Be fearless, dream big, and expect wonderful!

Chapter 17

Focus on Possibilities, Not Limitations

What is your first thought about any situation? If you are like most people, the first thing you'll notice are the limitations — the potential difficulties, what could go wrong, why it might not work out, etc. You might even catalog everything that could go wrong in your mind.

This insidious way of thinking has been referred to as "negativity bias" and it seems to infect most of us. This mindset is hugely miscreative because, by the Law of Attraction, what you focus on you attract. Which means you're more likely to experience those very difficulties and limitations! If you want to become a more deliberate creator, then you'll want to lose your habit of focusing on the negative and limitations and start focusing on the positive and possibilities instead!

The Buddha, who was deeply aware that we create our reality with our thoughts, aptly expressed the disempowering nature of this "limitation" mindset when he said: *"The mind that perceives the limitation is the limitation."*

Similar to the bad habit of focusing on limitations rather than possibilities, is the bad habit of focusing on "What Is" rather than "What Could Be" — a topic I explored in Never Mind What

Is, Imagine It the Way You Want It To Be. For better or worse, most of our thoughts are about things that we are observing — in other words about "What Is." Of course, by the Law of Attraction, letting "What Is" dominate your attention only serves to attract more of the same rather than something new. What you put your attention on is what you are thinking about, and what you predominately think about is what you'll get more of — that's the Law of Attraction in a nutshell.

The famous Law of Attraction teacher, Esther Hicks, put it this way:

> *Attention to WHAT IS only creates more WHAT IS.*
> *Look around less, imagine more.*

To powerfully create your reality more in alignment with your true desires, you must get better at ignoring what is and spend more time focusing on what could be. You must deliberately direct your thoughts rather than simply allowing what's happening around you dominate your attention.

The Power of Possibility Thinking

The weakness of the limitation mindset and the power of the possibility mindset was aptly pointed out by Mark Twain when he made this witty remark: *"They did not know it was impossible, so they did it."*

What if we ceased our insidious habit of always focusing on limitations, anticipating problems, and expecting the worst? And instead we primarily focused on possibilities and opportunities and consistently expected the best? What if we biased our thinking towards positivity, possibility, and opportunity? What if we adopted a tenacious habit of "possibility thinking" rather than habitual pessimism and "limitation thinking"?

The famous British statesman Winston Churchill commented on the difference between these two mindsets when he said:

> *A pessimist sees the difficulty in every opportunity; an optimist sees the opportunity in every difficulty.*

When you adopt a possibility mindset, what I assure you will happen is that things will start going your way far more often. Why? because by the Law of Attraction, your most predominant thoughts are your primary point of attraction. Which means a limitation mindset leads to experiencing more limitation, and a possibility mindset leads to the opposite.

Retrain your mind and watch the magic begin!

Chapter 18

The Power of the Spoken Word

Most people know that imagination and visualization are potent tools for powerful manifestation. But many are less familiar with the power of the spoken word and how their voice contributes to the creation of their reality. When you voice your thoughts, intentions, and desires, especially if you do so passionately, you add substantial energy to them and thereby dramatically increase the chances that they will manifest.

It might not be much of an exaggeration to say that your words are like orders placed with the universe, especially if you repeat the same words frequently and consistently and don't contradict them with conflicting thoughts, words, and deeds. Which by the way, is what most people are doing most of the time — having highly contradictory thoughts, words, and actions. That's why most people can't tell they are creating their reality — it's all canceling out, and the net effect is ambiguous and very little of their true desires ever manifest.

This point is eloquently hammered home by the renowned Law of Attraction teacher Abraham (as channeled by Esther Hicks) when he said...

When you no longer split your flow of energy with contradictory thoughts, you will know your power.

Before we dive into the power of the spoken word and how to apply it deliberately and effectively, I wanted to give you a little bit of the back-story of how I discovered my creatorship and the power of the spoken word.

Discovering My Creatorship

In the time since my "awakening" in the spring of 2014, the correlation between my thoughts, intentions, and desires and what shows up in my life has been blatantly obvious. One of the strange things that started happening during the early stages of my awakening, before I figured out what the heck was going on, was an amazing amount of synchronicities (very convenient "coincidences") and lots of "good luck."

My rational mind found it very strange because It didn't seem like it should be possible to be that lucky. It seemed like some kind of magic was going on or I was graced by the universe. Of course, when I stumbled upon The Law of Attraction it all clicked. All those convenient coincidences and good luck were a sign that I was powerfully creating my reality.

Needless to say, once you discover that you are creating your reality with your thoughts there's no going back. So, I dove into the study and application of the laws and mechanics of reality creation with a passion. I had a burning desire to become a master of manifestation! As I experimented with deliberate creation techniques, I routinely was manifesting undeniable results. Wow, this whole creator thing might be true! I considered the possibility that I might be going crazy but after discovering that many other people were reporting the same kind of thing, I decided I wasn't. Woooh! I really am a creator! And so is everyone else whether they know it or not!

Discovering the Power of the Spoken Word

One of the things I noticed, as I continued to experiment with and test my ability to manifest, was that every time I passionately voiced my desires out loud, they manifested incredibly fast! The results were often startling, the closest thing to real miracles and magic I've ever experienced!

Expressing a thought, intention, or desire verbally as words, regardless of who hears it, greatly amplifies its attractive/creative power. Even if you are the only one that hears it you are making a statement to the Universe and this is a very powerful act. With my first-hand experience of this it is now standard practice for me to passionately voice my desires and intentions out loud to the Universe on a regular basis.

Applying the Power of the Spoken Word Deliberately

There are a couple of ways that the power of your voice can be deliberately applied to enhance your creation efforts.

Adding Energy to Your Thoughts, Intentions, and Desires

The first one is pretty obvious. When you are thinking about your desires, and dreams, and intentions — and when you are deliberately imagining and visualizing them — also shout it out to the Universe. Be very expressive — say it strongly, say it passionately, say it loudly! Let the Universe know how you really feel! I now pretty much voice out loud every intention and desire of any consequence that I have. Try it and then pay attention to what shows up — you will be impressed.

To really let loose with some very passionate and energetic voicing of your desires and intentions you need to have adequate privacy. I often take walks alone in the woods and hills, and this provides a good time for me to share my deepest hopes and dreams with the Universe. Another time is when you are driving your car alone, which for most of us is fairly frequently, especially driving to and from work.

A part of the reason that voicing your intentions and desires enhances your manifestations is based on the principles of The Law of Attraction. The Law of Attraction states that the more focus, attention, and clarity you give a particular subject the more powerfully you will attract the essence of it into your reality and the more likely it is to appear in your life.

By having to put your intentions and desires into words, you are forced to formulate clear, concise, statements, and hence you're increasing their clarity. And by saying them, as well as thinking and imagining them, you're essentially repeating them which is also increasing the amount of focus and attention you are giving them.

And anytime you turn your thoughts, desires, intentions into words — either written or spoken — you are adding energy to them and thereby amplifying their manifestational power yet again.

How often should you think about and voice your intentions, desires, and dreams? Frequently, because as we said the amount of attention and focus you give a subject is one of the primary determinants of how fast and well it will manifest.

But be aware of two important things.

Don't try to voice your desires if you are **feeling down**. You only want to do this when you are in a very upbeat happy mood — when you are in a high vibration — because the higher your vibration, the more powerful the effect of focused intention and desire will be.

And **pay attention to how you feel** as you repeatedly voice your desires. You might unwittingly be bringing the subtle energy of fear and worry to the effort without realizing it if you are not attuned to your feelings. If you feel like you are repeating them because you are worried they might not come to pass, then doubt has crept in and is canceling out the positive effect of voicing your desires. Sometimes it may be better to voice your desires just a few times very strongly and then just relax, trust, and focus on something else.

And of course, to maximize your results you want to combine voicing your intentions and desires with **taking congruent action**. Action is the strongest form of intention and is a powerful attractor. And here's the great part, it almost doesn't matter what you do as long as you do something — small actions in the general direction of your intention or desire have a huge effect! Do you need to stress out about what actions to take? No, just follow your intuition — it's as simple as that. To dive deeper into the role of action in manifestation check these two chapters about action — Action Speaks Louder Than Words and The Role of Action in Manifestation.

Affirming Empowering Beliefs and Feelings

You can also employ the power of your spoken words by using the deliberate creation tool known as "Affirmations" (also sometimes called Mantras). While affirmations are a well-known and popular manifesting tool, they can also be one of the least effective, simply because many people are not aware of the correct way to utilize them.

Affirmations are statements (spoken or written) that are frequently repeated to help reinforce empowering beliefs and positive feelings. In effect, they can be used to dissolve old disempowering beliefs and install new empowering ones. This function of affirmations is of crucial importance because beliefs play a pivotal role in what you can manifest — your beliefs shape your thoughts and your thoughts shape your reality. To further explore this topic, check the chapter, Your Beliefs Shape Your Reality.

Another function of affirmations is to reinforce positive feelings. This function is very important because as you may know, your feelings and emotion is what contributes most of the energy to your thoughts and hence to the likelihood of their manifestation. Good feelings powerfully attract good things.

Affirmations are not "magical incantations" that will transform specific aspects of your life overnight. They simply gradually alter your predominant point of attraction because their regular repetition increases the amount of focus and attention you are giving to the empowering beliefs and feelings that those statements represent. It is just a systematic way of doing this making them a very powerful manifestation tool if used properly. Which is the subject of the next section.

Creating and Using Affirmations Effectively

There is a subtle art and science to the use of affirmations. Picking an affirmation out of a hat, or from a collection created by others, will not necessarily be appropriate or effective for you.

Affirmations are most effective when they are made highly specific to the individual. They should always be customized by you, for you. They should reflect your exact needs stated in your own words and your own way, and in a way that resonates with you deeply, for best results. This is the danger of using pre-created collections of affirmations — you may not realize that they need to be customized to fit you.

Also, the affirmations you use must be believable to you, or they won't work. This is another common pitfall of using affirmations. If the they are too bold or audacious (e.g; not believable) they won't be effective.

One of the main purposes of affirmations is to reprogram your subconscious beliefs. One of the reasons why they can do this is that as you repeatedly affirm a new belief, you will begin to attract experiences consistent with the new belief, which means you will begin to see evidence for the new belief. And seeing evidence will increase your confidence and any contradictory beliefs will begin to dissolve, and the new belief will begin to install.

But you are not going to reprogram your beliefs by repeatedly saying something that conflicts to strongly with your current beliefs. This is where the subtle art of creating effective affirmations comes in and where you can apply the technique that I call "bridging." A technique where you significantly tone down an affirmation and then gradually make it bolder as you become more confident. More about this in the next section.

How to Tell If an Affirmation Will Be Effective

You can tell if an affirmation will be effective by the way it makes you feel when you say it. If you feel comfortable saying it, or better yet, if you feel good — positive, uplifted, inspired, motivated, enthusiastic, optimistic, etc — then it's going to be effective.

If you don't feel comfortable when saying an affirmation — if you feel uneasy, anxious, uncomfortable, doubtful, pessimistic, or uninspired or neutral — it means that the affirmation conflicts with your existing beliefs too greatly, or triggers fears, or isn't targeting what you really desire. And this means that the affirmation is not going to work until you adjust it.

It's a fairly straightforward process to iteratively tweak an affirmation till its believable and it feels right. It's pretty simple because you can tell by how you feel when you say it — if it doesn't feel right keep tweaking it.

Here's an example of customizing and tweaking a confidence and success related affirmation. Here it is in its boldest form:

I am a capable and successful person. Everything I do turns to gold.

How does that make you feel? If you are like many people, who have low self-worth and who struggle to be successful saying this will likely make you feel uneasy. Here is an example of how to tweak it to make it more believable feel better.

I am learning to become more confident that I'm a capable person every day. My success is increasing every day as I believe in myself and my dreams.

Can you feel the difference? Get the idea? The book The Power of Affirmations & The Secret to Their Success provides other great examples and further instruction that will help you better understand how to create an effective affirmation so check that out if you want to dive deeper into this subject.

Maximizing the Power of Your Affirmations

How often to say your affirmations? Frequently — at least once a day for a while, perhaps less as it becomes more ingrained. Remember that by the Law of Attraction the amount of attention and focus you give a subject is one of the primary determinants of how fast and well something manifests. Your repetition of the affirmation is more time focused on the subject of the affirmation making it a much more powerful attractor.

How to say your affirmations for best results? Say them with as much passion, energy, conviction, and emotion as you can muster. The amount of emotion and energy you express when saying an affirmation makes them proportionally more powerful. And makes them dramatically more powerful than If you say them flatly!

If you are having a hard time mustering enthusiasm when saying an affirmation, it might be because it is too bold and not believable to you, or perhaps not what you really desire, and you should consider revising it until enthusiasm comes naturally when you say it. But believe it or not, faking it is Okay. If you can suspend your disbelief and muster something that feels like genuine enthusiasm when you say your affirmation, then more power to you!

When and where to say your affirmations? Anytime where you have adequate privacy to express yourself strongly. Find those alone times and use them. And remember, don't do your affirmations if you are feeling down. You only want to say them when you are in a very upbeat happy mood — this is when they will have the best effect.

Diving Deeper into Mastering Affirmations

If you'd like to dive deeper into this topic, then I highly recommend the book The Power of Affirmations & The Secret to Their Success. It explores the subtleties and nuances of creating and using affirmations effectively and includes a huge collection of them covering areas such as wealth and abundance, health and well-being, happiness and confidence, love and relationships, and success and career. Anyone thinking about adding affirmations to their deliberate creation toolbox should read this book first.

Examples of Applying the Power of the Spoken Word

So, to help you better understand deliberate creation and applying the power of the spoken word here are a few personal examples from my own experience.

Dinner in Sedona

One of my most startling manifestations — bordering on the miraculous — happened when I was visiting Sedona Arizona (USA) for a week. I went down there to attend a week-long spiritual retreat and to sight-see. I went low budget and stayed in a campground and mostly ate out of a cooler with provisions purchased at the grocery store. Besides attending the retreat, I did a bunch of hiking in the beautiful desert mountains.

One day near the end of my trip I heard about a restaurant called "The Paleo Grill." It served grilled meals including vegetables and fish, foul, or beef. That sounded really good to me, and I decided that I'd treat myself to a dinner out before I left town.

On the day before my last day in Sedona, I went on a big all-day hike of one of the tallest mountains overlooking town. On the way up the mountain, I decided that I would go out to dinner that evening — to the Paleo Grill. But I had a bit of a problem — I wasn't sure if I had enough time for dinner out. Some friends I had met at the campground had invited me to hang out in the pool with them that evening, and the pool closed at 8 pm. I wasn't going to finish the hike till around 6:30 pm and it was a 30-minute drive back to the campground. If I stopped for a sit-down dinner at the restaurant, I might not make it back to the pool before it closed, and I'd miss the pool party. I also felt a little guilty about eating meat because I was trying to go vegan.

So there I was hiking down the mountain in the late afternoon thinking about my desire to have a nice meal of grilled meat and vegetables and still making the pool party before it ended. And as I often do, I started voicing my thoughts and desires out loud in a very animated and heartfelt way. Here's what I said as I talked to myself and the Universe:

---

*"I'm really looking forward to a nice meal of grilled meat and vegetables this evening. I've been real thrifty on this trip, and **I deserve** at least one dinner out on the town. I feel a little guilty about it because I'm trying to go vegan but heck, in the bigger picture there is no right and wrong, good or bad, so if I want to enjoy some grilled meat this evening there's nothing wrong with that — **I allow** myself to have this. But I don't want to miss the pool party either. And I'm not sure there's enough time to do both. **How can I have dinner and make the pool party? Is there a way?**"*

When I finally reached the trailhead parking lot, I noticed that there was a man and a woman sitting at a picnic table with a barbeque grill. I waved and smiled. They lifted their wine glasses and shouted something to me I didn't quite hear, so I went over to say hello.

When I got within ear-shot, they said: Want a glass of wine? I'm not a big wine fan, but somehow, I knew that I should go with the flow and so I said Heck Ya! and I sat down at their picnic table as they poured me a glass of wine and we introduced ourselves. It turned out that I had crossed paths with a delightful French family on a road trip of America.

After our brief but very cordial introductory chat, they immediately asked Would you like to have dinner with us? It's ready now — grilled steak and corn and a salad — do you like? With a big shit-eating grin on my face, I said Heck ya! I'd love to join you for dinner!

This was it — the fulfillment of my desire! And in a way that I would never have imagined! A home cooked grilled meal in a beautiful outdoor setting with a delightful French family — what could be better than that! And the dinner was ready as I arrived which meant that all the overhead of a sit-down meal at a restaurant — waiting to order, waiting for it to be prepared and served, etc. — was missing and I would make my pool party in time! The Universe had delivered the perfect solution to my desires and fast! Can you say, "Instant Manifestation?"

I manifest my desires all the time, but this was indeed one of the most impressive. Can you see the connection between the approach I took and the results? When was the last time I was invited to an impromptu barbeque dinner by strangers — NEVER! So, the correlation between my desire and the statement of my desire and this dinner arriving is an indisputable example of manifestation.

This experience poignantly illustrates many important aspects of powerful manifesting. (1) Passionately thinking and **voicing** your desires. (2) **Allowing** their fulfillment by releasing any blocks to receiving — e.g. undeservedness, unworthiness, limiting beliefs, etc. Note that I explicitly **affirmed** that **I deserved** a nice grilled dinner and that I would allow myself to have it **despite a potential limiting belief** that eating meat was "bad." (3) I **did not assume it wasn't possible** and **I didn't insist on HOW** it should or could happen. I was open to a possible solution and left the "how" to the universe by asking the question *"How can I have my grilled dinner and make the pool party too? Is there a way?"*

> *They did not know it was impossible, so they did it.* — Mark Twain

This is how the magic works! And of course, it's not really magic. You exist within something very much like a virtual reality and your every thought is attracting what appears on the screen that you call your life! This is just how creation works.

Finding a New Apartment

Here's another personal example of how to apply the power of the spoken word to deliberate creation.

I recently was asked to leave the apartment I was renting due to an indiscretion (which will remain anonymous), and I was worried that it would make finding a new apartment very difficult — because my "reason for leaving" was something that was going to be difficult for me to admit and hence I wouldn't have a reference for my last place of residence. And I already felt like I had one handicap which made it more difficult to find apartments (which I won't get into) and now had another. So, I was quite worried that I might not be able to find an apartment within the 30 days' notice that I had been given. I also was worried it might make it harder to find a place that I really liked.

I realized that the main problem in manifesting a new apartment would be my belief that I had these two major handicaps that might make it harder to find a new apartment. So, I attacked these limiting beliefs with the following affirmation:

I am a creator. I can create anything I can imagine and believe. I give no credence to the perceived handicaps to finding a new apartment — they are only valid if I believe they are. And I know that they are not because I know that I am creating my reality absolutely without exception based on my beliefs, thoughts, desires, and intentions.

I also realized I needed to put out a strong, clear vision of what I wanted so I also passionately voiced and envisioned the kind of new place I was looking for:

"I desire a quiet, peaceful, cozy country apartment preferably with a view of the mountains and a walk in a field or a woods nearby far from lights so I can see the stars at night clearly."

This is how I deliberately combined a strong affirmation of unlimitedness with painting a powerful picture of what I desired. And I repeated it three or four times, over the course of a week, while I was on evening walks under the stars and while driving my car. And the results were astounding! Within two days of completing those affirmations I stumbled upon an apartment that matched what I had envisioned and more. Not only did it have everything I had deliberately imagined but it also had a major feature that in hindsight I had been thinking about for over a month but hadn't included in my deliberate imagining and voicing. And get this, from the time I called the apartment owner till the time I had the keys in my hands was less than 1 hour and not a single question asked — Slam dunk!

Everything goes my way, hooray, hooray! I get everything I want and more, galore, galore!

And here's a very interesting side note to this experience that poignantly illustrates the importance of action and trust in powerful manifestation.

When I started looking at apartments, I must have looked at 5 or 6, and I hadn't filled out an application for any of them. Part of the reason was that none of them were a very good match to my desires but also, if I was honest with myself, I was afraid to because I wasn't sure how I was going to handle the "reason for leaving" question. I didn't want to lie but I also felt very uncomfortable with telling the truth. So even though I was taking action via going out there and looking at apartments, it wasn't fully committed action because I wasn't filling out any applications.

But then the first great opportunity appeared (the serendipity was startling, but I won't digress) but I was terrified to fill out and submit the application because I still didn't know what I was going to do with the "reason for leaving" question. For the remainder of the day, I dragged my feet and delayed. That evening I got a very clear and amusingly delivered symbolic message from the Universe. In a nutshell, the message was this — TRUST. (Did I mention that I have a strong connection with my higher-self and my spirit guides? "The Angels, the Masters, and the Universe" as I sometimes refer to them? But that's another story — which I might write more about sometime.)

I laughed, and I said out loud: *"Yes, of course, trust and faith are the keys to powerful manifesting. Thanks for the reminder."* This was my guides way of letting me know that I was very close to manifesting my desired results and a hint to take committed action — e.g; fill out an application, tell the truth, and to trust that everything would work out fine. So I decided to tell the absolute truth about my "reason for leaving" on every apartment application that I filled out and just trust the Universe and let the chips fall where they may.

Which is what I did the next morning when I filled out my very first apartment application and emailed it. Not more than 5 seconds had passed after sending that first application when my intuition told me I should check the craigslist apartment listings again. My jaw dropped when I saw that the very first item in the "apartments for rent" listing was a beautiful log cabin in the country near the mountains just as I had been envisioning. Needless to say, I called immediately. *"Can you come over now?"* they said. *"Heck ya!"* I replied. And guess what? In less than one hour I had the keys to that place, no questions asked!

It was almost like the moment I confessed my sins the universe rewarded me by instantly dropping the apartment of my dreams into my lap. Of course, it had very little to do with confessing my sins, and much more to do with committed action and trust. I had finally filled out an application and sent it! That committed action was the signal to the Universe of my serious intent and desire. As soon as I committed, a perfect opportunity appeared instantly! Also, by choosing to tell the truth no matter what, I was sending a strong signal to the Universe that I trusted it to deliver my desire! Wow! That's one hell of a lesson on how committed action and trust influence the outcome of your manifestations!

Affirming Your Creatorship

Ok, here's an affirmation that I thought would be pertinent to share here. This affirmation could be considered the mantra of powerful creators. It targets the root of your creational power by reinforcing your belief in your creatorship and reminding yourself of the key elements of powerful manifestation. Here it is.

I am a creator. I am creating my personal reality with my thoughts, beliefs, focus, and more. I create my reality absolutely without exception regardless of whether I understand how, and hence I take full responsibility for everything that enters my direct experience. I exist within a field of infinite possibilities — whatever I can imagine and believe can come to pass. TRUST and faith are the key. I do not concern myself with HOW things will come to pass. I simply envision the desired outcome, take inspired action, and trust that it will appear in my reality at the perfect time in the perfect way.

This is a bold, perhaps even audacious, affirmation of one's creatorship. Depending on where you are at with mastering manifestation and your creatorship you may not be ready for one this bold. Just understanding the theory of the Law of Attraction is not enough. If you haven't noticed the correlations between your spontaneous or deliberate thoughts, intentions, and desires and what has been appearing in your life then likely this affirmation will simply not be believable and hence will not be effective.

This affirmation might be good to say when dealing with challenging situations involving apparent limitations or constraints to remind yourself that all perceived limitations are only operative if you believe them, and that by giving them no credence you can manifest best-case outcomes.

As an example of an alternative creatorship affirmation more appropriate for a beginner consider this:

I am learning to become a powerful deliberate creator. Every day I am noticing more poignant examples of how my thoughts, intentions, and desires are correlated with what appears in my life. Every day I'm becoming more convinced that I am indeed creating my reality absolutely without exception. Every day I am becoming a more masterful deliberate creator.

Believe it or not, this affirmation will attract information and experiences to you that will help you become a more confident and powerful deliberate creator. And at some point, you will have the confidence to assuredly recite the bolder version of the creator affirmation that I offered.

Or perhaps you'll prefer to chant this delightful, lighthearted, tongue-in-cheek creatorship affirmation:

Everything goes my way, hooray, hooray! I get everything I want and more, galore, galore!

More power to you!

Chapter 19

The Role of Action in Manifestation

Many people misunderstand the role of action in creating the results they are getting in their lives. Those that are unaware that their reality is a construct and that it is dynamically generated from the essence of their own thoughts and beliefs (and more), generally think that action is the ONLY thing that is causing the results they are getting.

But of course, there's a lot more going on under the hood, and I'm going to explore it in this article. This isn't the first time I've written about this topic, check the chapter, Action Speaks Louder Than Words for more about the role of action in manifestation. The reason I'm revisiting this topic is to take a look at it from a new angle that I think will be very helpful in understanding and mastering deliberate creation.

So, without further ado, let's dive in.

Action, Results, and Cause and Effect

As I have said, those who are unaware of The Law of Attraction believe that the ONLY way to get results is through action. And there is no denying that action causes results. Taking a certain action in a certain situation produces a certain result — the action DIRECTLY causes an effect or result — this is what is known as Linear Cause and Effect.

But action also INDIRECTLY causes effects via the Law of Attraction, in the same way as your thoughts, desires, and intentions do — a process that might be called Non-linear Cause and Effect. And the indirect effects of action are not produced by the action, per se, but by the desire and intention that inspired the action.

Action Amplifies Your Desires and Intentions

Taking action serves to amplify the root desire and intention that sponsored the action. And then, by the Law of Attraction, the strengthened intention more powerfully attracts circumstances that will facilitate the attainment of the root desire. This is why I often say "action is the strongest form of intention."

Every action is inspired by or sponsored by, a root desire and intention, and thus action represents a powerful concrete expression of the sponsoring desire and intention. And this adds substantial energy to the root desire and intention which then more powerfully attracts events, circumstances, people, information, and things that can serve as opportunities to the fulfillment of the desire.

An Example of the Non-Linear Effects of Action

So, here's a recent experience that I think poignantly illustrates how action can indirectly manifest results via the Law of Attraction. I shared the complete story of this experience in a recent article on my website, which you may find interesting and helpful to read, but I'll share the gist of it (that pertains to the point I'm trying make) here.

Manifesting a New Apartment

Recently I was forced to find a new apartment. And I had reason to believe, and was worried, that I might have a hard time finding one (but I won't get into the reason why here). I knew that it would be important to do some deliberate creation work to neutralize my fears and focus on what I wanted. So, I envisioned the apartment of my dreams, and I affirmed reasons why it should be easy to find multiple times over the course of a week.

After searching for about a week, I had visited four or five apartment prospects but hadn't submitted an application for any of them because, for one thing, they weren't quite what I was looking for. Then the first passable prospect showed up — not my dream apartment, but I could live with it — and so I filled out the application and submitted it to the property manager. This is the action that I am using for this example.

Now, of course submitting an apartment application, by linear cause and effect is going to result in either an acceptance or rejection of the application. You either get the apartment, or you don't. So if my application was accepted and I got the apartment you might say that my action of submitting the application caused the final manifestation of the apartment.

But I didn't get a chance to find out which outcome of that action would come to pass because within seconds of submitting the application, and before the apartment's property manager could have even seen it, a completely different apartment prospect unexpectedly appeared that was the absolute perfect match to my desires! Taking the committed action of submitting an application instantly triggered the manifestation of my dream apartment, essentially out of the blue.

I was stunned and delighted, and immediately seized the opportunity by calling the owner, and I closed the deal miraculously quickly — I had the keys to the new place in my hands less than 1 hour after submitting the application for the other apartment! And only one and a half weeks after starting my apartment search which is dramatically faster than any other apartment search, I've done in recent times.

This was very close to a best-case outcome, and this is the kind of result you can expect when you master deliberate creation!

Action Isn't the Only Thing that Amplifies Your Desires and Intentions

And of course, it isn't just your actions that can add energy to and amplify your desires and intentions — your thoughts and words (and emotions) also can. If your thoughts and words are congruent (e.g; aligned) with your desires and intentions, then you are amplifying them and hence their attractive power. But if you think and say things that are incongruent with (or contradictory to) your desires and intentions then you are reducing their attractive power, and hence they are less likely to manifest — in fact, you might completely negate them and completely block their manifestation.

This point is echoed in the following statement made by Abraham via Esther Hicks:

> When you no longer split your flow of energy
> with **contradictory thoughts**, you will know **your**
> **power.**

And believe it or not, this is happening all the time because most people's thoughts and words are contradicting their desires and intentions alarmingly frequently — and they aren't even aware of it! Have you noticed most people are habitually pessimistic? Most people chronically worry, anticipate problems, expect the worst, focus on what they don't want, etc. — and this is all very mis-creative.

Action Is Not the Primary Tool of Manifesting

Action is an essential ingredient to powerfully manifesting your desires and intentions, but it is not the primary tool or the only tool. It's also not the first step in the manifestation process. The best way to understand the role of action in manifestation is that it is just one of many ingredients that we must apply correctly to powerfully manifest our desires.

The mistake that most people make, those that are not aware that they are creating their reality with their thoughts, is that they ONLY use action to create and they don't realize that their thoughts, beliefs, etc. are paving the way for all their manifestations.

If you believe that the only way you get results in your life is through action and you don't pave the way with clear desires and intentions and positive expectations, then getting the results that you desire is going to require far more effort than if you understand that your thoughts are paving the way.

Your thoughts are far more important than the action you take — they are what is setting the stage — one that is either highly conducive to the fulfillment of your desires or one that is not. Part of the reason for this is that your thoughts (and beliefs etc.)

are active every minute of every day and therefore a constant point of attraction whereas your actions are just short-lived momentary events.

This point is echoed in the statement below by the non-physical being Abraham (through Esther Hicks):

What you DO is miniscule in comparison with what you choose to THINK, because your vibration is so much more powerful and so much more important.

When you pave the way with your thoughts, you will find (if you are paying attention) that circumstances will appear, through synchronicity and serendipity, that will facilitate the attainment of your desires and intentions. And this generally means that far less effort will be required. Action is still an essential ingredient, but there will be more inspired action and less brute force action.

How Much Action is Required?

How much action is required for optimal results? Well, that depends, because not all manifestations require the same amount of action to bring them to fruition. Certain desires will not need very little action for them to fully manifest. Others will need many actions to fully manifest. It depends on whether the desire is trivial or non-trivial to manifest.

In this regard, it is useful to distinguish two major categories of manifestation; (1) single-step manifestations and (2) multi-step manifestations.

Single-Step Manifestations

Single step manifestations are relatively simple and require only a single action step to fully attain the desired result. A typical example is when you've been strongly desiring a certain thing then the perfect opportunity to have that thing appears, and the only action that is required might be to make the purchase, or to accept the gift, or call the person that has it, etc. and then you've got your end result.

Sometimes it might even appear that there was no action involved at all. For example, let's say the shirts in your wardrobe collection are all wearing thin and you've frequently been thinking about (strongly desiring) getting some new ones. Then unexpectedly, and for whatever reason, a friend gifts you with some shirts that they found on sale. Virtually no action was required, only accepting the gift!

Here's a personal example of a single-step manifestation.

Example of Single-Step manifestation

Recently a friend of mine visited me to do some ice climbing and backcountry skiing. We had four days, and we thought we might do three days of ice climbing and one day of backcountry skiing. The weather wasn't cooperating very well. We were having a heinous warm spell which was affecting both the ice and snow. We did manage to find enough intact ice to enjoy, but the snow conditions were abysmal — very unpleasant skiing conditions — and probably not worth going skiing.

But I had never skied with my friend in Montana, and I was really looking forward to showing him a good time skiing. Also, I didn't want to ice climb four days in a row — just two tiring and monotonous. So, I had a very strong desire to go skiing, and during every one of the first three days as we were ice climbing in the back of my mind I was repeatedly thinking *"Gosh I really want to go skiing I really want to show my friend a good time out in the snow."*

But the conditions were completely abysmal for skiing, and there was absolutely no prognosis from the forecast that that situation would change — no new snow in sight. So, there was the appearance that skiing was out of the question. But I just kept wishing for it in the back of my mind and low and behold at the end of the 3rd day of ice climbing the forecast changed unexpectedly to some snow moving in late that night. Of course, I say "unexpected" with a grin on my face because things go my way unexpectedly a lot. So, I just smiled and said to my friend *"It looks like we're going skiing tomorrow, hallelujah!"*

That evening before going to bed the snow hadn't started yet. But I just stated my desire again to go skiing in reasonably good conditions, imagined ourselves doing luscious powder turns and set my intention to assume that the skiing was going to be good and just get up in the morning and put the skis in the car and go.

And of course, when we woke up in the morning there was a bit of fresh snow on the ground in town which meant there'd be enough new snow up in the mountains to have fun. So, we took the committed action of putting our skis in the car, getting in, and driving to the trailhead in the mountains. And of course, the snow turned out to be good and the skiing thoroughly enjoyable! Slam dunk!

So, as you can see this manifestation took only one action step — simply seizing the opportunity when it arrived. And manifesting many of your desires, especially the smaller stuff, will be this simple. But others will not and will require consistent and persistent application of deliberate creation techniques as well as action. This is the subject of the next section.

Multi-Step Manifestations

Like I've said, certain non-trivial desires will require a series of steps and more than one action to fully manifest. A typical example of this type is the manifestation of your big dreams and desires.

To powerfully manifest these kinds of desires the best approach, in terms of action, is to take many small action steps on a consistent basis. Not only will these action steps create results via linear cause and effect that will bring you ever closer to the full manifestation of your desire or dream. But they will also amplify the root desire and intention and hence attract, via the Law of Attraction, circumstances, people, information, and even inspiration and knowledge straight from divine intelligence that will further facilitate the attainment of your desire or dream.

And here's the good part. It doesn't really matter what actions you take as long as they are heading in the general direction of your desire or dream. Just start taking baby steps, and the Law of Attraction will bring you the information, inspiration, and guidance that will help you adjust your course.

Realize for every little step you take, you increase, exponentially, what the Universe can do for you.

— Mike Dooley, <u>Playing the Matrix</u>

You just start taking action to demonstrate in the strongest possible way that you are serious about attaining your desire or dream. The universe will then provide the guidance that will eventually lead you to its full attainment if you (1) have trust and faith, (2) pay attention for the opportunities and guidance that it will send your way, and (3) act on them.

Here's a hypothetical and typical example of this type of manifestation — the attainment of a big dream.

Example of a Multi-Step Manifestation

Here's a hypothetical example. Let's say your big dream is to be a Rock Superstar. You're not going to go from someone who doesn't know how to read music and doesn't know how to play the guitar to rock superstar by taking only one action. Nobody is going to call you with a big record contract without some intermediary steps to acquire the pertinent skills.

In the case of wanting to become a Rock Superstar the first action, you'll probably want to take is to learn how to read music. Then perhaps the next action is to learn how to play the guitar. And perhaps the next action we'll be to find some gigs performing at some small local venues. You get the idea.

With consistent actions, however small, in the general direction of your dream serendipitous opportunities will appear that lead you to hit the big time. The more that you can clearly envision, feel, and believe in your destiny as a Rock Superstar the sooner it will come.

And it will likely unfold in the form of curious unexpected and fortuitous events leading eventually to a major opportunity that when seized takes you all the way to your desired end result — being the Rock Superstar you always knew you would be.

At this point, you might be wondering why it is relatively difficult to manifest our big dreams and desires — they tend to take many steps over a significant amount of time. Why can't we just manifest our big dreams more quickly? The short answer is that it's by design — we wanted to experience journeys of becoming.

Journeys of Becoming

In the non-physical, we can manifest anything, however simple or complex, in a single step by thought and desire alone. In the physical this is not the case — physical reality is a time and space construct and that implies motion and action. In the physical, we wanted to experience action and we wanted to experience journeys of becoming, and all the qualities associated with that — such as perseverance, determination, courage, etc.

And hence we designed this reality construct to allow ourselves to experience highly formative and rewarding journeys of becoming — and they are unlike anything that we can experience in the non-physical realms of existence. We are completely responsible for creating those journeys and what we want to become but anything that we can imagine, believe, and demonstrate consistent strong intention for we can become!

This truth was eloquently expressed by the British philosophical writer, James Allen, when he said:

> *Dream lofty dreams, and as you dream, so you shall become. Your vision is the promise of what you shall one day be; your ideal is the prophecy of what you shall at last unveil.*

We wanted these journeys to be somewhat challenging to manifest because we didn't want to rob ourselves of the important qualities, we could learn from them, or the exhilaration we could experience from them, by making them too easy. The higher non-physical aspect of yourself has access to all the knowledge, skills, and wisdom of Source already and wanted to experience having to gain them through desire, effort, persistence, and courage.

In the higher realms, we already have access to all the knowledge and skills needed for whatever we can imagine. In the higher realms, we can manifest whatever we can imagine with only our thoughts and do it instantly. We didn't create this reality construct to be easy — we created it to be interesting and challenging — and hence formative.

If you have a strong enough desire to become something, and you are willing to take congruent action, and to believe in yourself you can become anything! Why? Because you will summon all the skills and capabilities you need from Source — from divine intelligence! Your strong desire and committed actions are part of what brings forth the knowledge, skills, and capabilities that are available within Source. Source is within you and wants to express your dream through you!

Living your dream is the greatest gift you can give to the world. There is nothing higher.

— Story Waters

But this requires substantial desire, substantial belief and faith, substantial intention and the strongest form of intention is action! That's why one of the six rules of success offered by the great achiever Arnold Schwarzenegger is "Work like hell!" And even though you should use your thoughts to pave the way to any successful manifestation this rule of thumb from Arnold definitely has a lot of validity for achieving one's big dreams.

Arnold's Six Rules of Success

With all the success that Arnold Schwarzenegger has achieved he's clearly a very powerful deliberate creator. So, it might be smart to pay attention to his advice about success and attaining your dreams.

1. Trust yourself

2. Break some rules

3. Don't be afraid to fail

4. Ignore the naysayers

5. Work your butt off

6. Give Something back

Self-Creatorship Mantra

Since we're on the topic of becoming here's an affirmation that can help you to transcend your limiting self-concepts and become a more powerful self-creator. It is a bold, even audacious, affirmation that reminds us that we are not only creating our reality but also ourselves, with our every thought, word, and deed. And it reminds us that we are all expressions of Source consciousness and can tap into the knowledge and wisdom that it holds to become whatever we can imagine and believe.

I am a creator. I'm not only creating my reality with my thoughts and beliefs but I'm also creating MYSELF. Not only can I HAVE anything I desire but I can BE anything I desire. I can BECOME whatever I can imagine and believe. With sufficient desire, intention, and action I can summon everything I need from Source to become ANYTHING I choose. I release all limiting self-concepts because I KNOW that with persistence and faith Source will express through me any and all knowledge and skills required for me to become whatever I desire.

This affirmation and everything I've said about "becoming" might seem a bit pie-in-the-sky, but keep in mind that I'm not saying becoming anything you desire will be easy. Of course, becoming something extra-ordinary will require extra-ordinary desire, clarity, mental discipline, and effort. I'm just saying it is possible to become whatever you can imagine, believe, and strongly desire.

There is nothing limiting yourself but yourself — your own beliefs, attitudes, habits, etc. Of course, becoming something extra-ordinary will require an appropriate mindset and habits.

Summing It All Up

So, to sum it all up here are the key points. Action is but one of many ingredients for the powerful manifestation of your desires. Action is essential to the manifestation of your desires, especially your big dreams, yet it is far less important than your thoughts (and your attitudes and beliefs). Your thoughts are creating your predominant point of attraction and hence are paving the way for the manifestation of your desires and hence should be considered the primary tool of manifestation.

Yet for manifesting everything except trivial (simple to manifest) desires the best approach is to consistently take small actions (baby steps) in the general direction of your desire. Doing this moves you closer to the fulfillment of your desire by linear cause and effect and also amplifies the sponsoring desire and intention behind the actions and hence more powerfully attracts (via non-linear cause and effect) circumstances, information, people, and inspiration that will facilitate the fulfillment of your desire. And always be on the lookout for the opportunities that you manifest and seize them!

Chapter 20

The Power of Gratitude and Appreciation

I've written about the power of gratitude and appreciation before in chapter <u>Notice and Appreciate Every Little Good Thing in Your Life</u> but this subject is so important that I decided to revisit it.

Appreciation and Gratitude Pave the Way for Abundance

If you didn't know anything about The Law of Attraction, if you didn't know any of the principles of Deliberate Creation and you just used this one practice — regularly expressing gratitude — you'd be way ahead of the game. The bottom line is, regularly taking notice of the stuff in your life and the world that you like, and expressing appreciation and gratitude for it, attracts more of the same into your life.

The attitude of gratitude attracts more good thing into your life.

The opposite of this practice is the insidious habit of routinely noticing what you don't like. This is a very common habit. Most people seem to have a habitual bias of noticing and complaining about the things they see around them that they don't like. And sadly, most of them are completely unaware that they are doing it and how miscreative it is.

If you know anything about The Law of Attraction, then you know that what you think about and you give attention to you attract. And this is why there's power in gratitude and appreciation — not because God wants or needs you to be appreciative of its creations and not because gratitude is "good". But simply because gratitude and appreciation has you focusing on what you like — and what you give more attention to, you are more likely to attract into your life. It's that simple. That's how The Law of Attraction works.

> *If all you did was just look for things to appreciate you would live a joyous, spectacular life. Become a person who appreciates, and you will thrive!*
>
> — Abraham via <u>Esther Hicks</u>

And this isn't the only reason why gratitude is such a powerful deliberate creation practice. It isn't just a matter of where you are putting your attention and what you are thinking about.

Emotion Amplifies Attraction

It's also the strength of the emotion associated with what you're thinking about and giving attention too. The emotion associated with a thought greatly amplifies its attractive power. And the emotion of appreciation and gratitude is a very strong positive emotion. That's why gratitude is so powerful — it has you expressing strong positive emotion as you focus on what you like.

Learning to Focus on What You Like Rather than What You Don't

One of the benefits of a regular gratitude practice, besides what I've already mentioned, is that it can help you eliminate whatever tendency you have to focus on what you don't like. When you regularly and deliberately and consciously make an effort to notice the things around you in your own life or in other people's lives, and the world at large, that you like you are leaving less time to focus on what you don't like. By the way, what you choose to focus on is one of the key deliberate creation principles which I have explored in depth in the chapter Focus on What You Want, Not What You Don't.

In addition to diverting your attention to more productive targets, once you get in the habit of noticing what you like and getting familiar with the good feeling of appreciation, then when you inadvertently start paying attention to something you don't like and start complaining it will stand out like a sore thumb. Why? Because the feeling that you have when you're focusing on what you don't like is very different than the good feelings associated with the state of appreciation. When you are putting your attention on something you don't like (and perhaps bitching, moaning, and complaining about it) you don't feel good. This enables you to catch yourself focusing on what you don't like — by noticing how you feel.

When you feel those negative feelings and you realize you're that you're complaining you can just stop immediately and even better switch to expressing gratitude for something else. In this way you can reprogram yourself away from habitually paying attention to what you don't like. Which is very important to do because whatever you focus on you increase the probability of experiencing. If you pay a lot of attention to what you don't like, then you are increasing the chances you will get more of what you don't like!

The sad truth is that most of the time most of the people are simply blocking the manifestation of their true desires via their miscreative habits of thinking. And the practice of regularly noticing and expressing appreciation for the good things in your life and in the world offer one step in the right direction.

Building a Gratitude Practice

Set aside some time on a regular basis where you can deliberately look for things to express gratitude for. They don't have to be big things. In fact, it's all the little stuff that makes up the very fabric of your life.

Don't underestimate how all the little stuff contributes to your happiness. You can do your gratitude sessions anytime you have a few free minutes and can do them anywhere if you just say thanks in the sanctity of your own mind. But of course, if you say it out loud you add a lot of energy and power to it so this is preferable. A few places I've found were I can state my gratitude (or intentions, desire, and hopes and dreams) out loud to the universe are when I'm driving around in my car by myself and also on my evening walks under the stars. You might think of some other ideas.

The **attitude of gratitude** is a powerful deliberate creation tool that every master creator is very adept at.

More power to you!

Chapter 21

The Power of Prayer and the Power of Love

I wanted to share a recent experience that I had that I consider a profound and poignant example of the power of prayer and the power of love. The background to the story is that last fall I met a new friend who I started rock climbing with, and when the winter set in, I introduced him to ice climbing. I'm an avid ice climber, and I was showing him the ropes of ice climbing. We went out ice climbing regularly, almost once a week, and the first time we went out my friend asked if he could bring his dog, and I said *"Yeah why not, I love dogs. Bring your dog."*

His dog's named Missy. She's 77 years old in human years. But the dog is super fit super spry and has an incredible curiosity and energy and a keen sense of intelligence and just loves being outside in the mountains. Very often we couldn't get her to get back in the car. She didn't want to leave the mountains. She just loved being out there. This story is related to the dog.

As a curious side note, the funny thing is that the dog is almost like the dog version of me. The dog is old yet very fit and spry and energetic and has a keen curiosity and loves the mountains.

Well, I'm kind of old, I just turned 60, and I'm fit and spry and very energetic and loved the mountains too. So that's just the weird side note. Anyways back to the story.

So, I fell in love with Missy. I just love the dog, and Neil loves the dog and wanted the dog to come out and really enjoy the outdoors with us. So about four weeks ago I'm walking home from a walk, and I crossed paths with my friend, and he tells me that he lost Missy. And I say, *"What do you mean you lost Missy?"*

He said that he had been out on a back-country mountain ski tour with his friends and they brought Missy. They summited a 10,000-foot snow covered jagged peak called Blackmore Peak, and when they were at the summit, the dog saw some mountain goats way down on the other side of the mountain and took off after them. They couldn't get the dog back. It was late in the day the terrain was very rugged and treacherous down there, and they just didn't have time. And they eventually had to leave without the dog.

I met up with him when he just was on his way home. So, with my positive attitude, I said something positive. I said, *"She'll be alright, I think she's going to find her way out because she is such a fit and smart and outdoor savvy dog. I'm pretty sure she's going to do fine and find her way out and end up with somebody if it's not us."*

That evening I was on another walk, and I decided to say a prayer for Missy. I told the universe that I dearly loved Missy and that if it wasn't her time to go will you please assist and guide her out of the mountains to someone that could love her. That was my prayer. About three days later I was going out to the mountains by myself to do a back-country ski-tour. I had completely forgotten about the fact that Missy was still lost. I was just excited to get out on a ski tour.

I was driving to the trail-head in the mountains and about two-thirds of the way to the trail-head there is a bridge across a dam, and it was completely blocked by very large snowdrifts. We had had a snow storm and had been windy, so I wasn't able to cross the bridge and get to the trail-head so I was forced to pick an alternative destination which was a trail-head that was just on my side of the bridge. Which just so happens to be the trail to the peak that the dog was lost on, although I wasn't in my mind, I had completely forgotten about that. But anyways and it was really my only option now that I couldn't make it to the place I had planned on.

So, I chose to ski up what is called the Blackmore Mountain trail which is about five miles and 4000 feet to the summit. I was the only one who had been up this trail that day, and it was beautiful untracked fresh powder and sunshine   a very beautiful day and I'm about halfway to the summit skiing along up the hill, and I heard or felt something behind me, and I turned around.

As I turned around there was a dog standing in the trail — it was
Missy!

It was then that I remembered that I had said a prayer for Missy
and realized the universe had blocked the bridge because it
knew that the only thing that I would choose to do under those
conditions is to go up the Blackmore Mountain trail. It knew
that's what I would choose. It was guiding me to intersect with
Missy. Why do I say this? Guess how many times I have been up
this road and crossed that dam and bridge? Hundreds of times
over the last 15 years maybe thousand times. And guess how
many times the bridge was impassable? Yep, you guessed it zero
times! This is the only time the bridge has ever been impassable
in the hundreds of times that I've gone up this road. So the
universe conspired to block the bridge knowing that my only
choice would be to go up that trail and I would intersect with
the dog. But wait, it gets better!

Now I kind of wanted to continue up the mountain. But the dog
had been outside for two nights and almost three whole days in
full winter conditions in the high peaks of Montana! I certainly
wasn't going to make the dog go back up the mountain. It had
to be tired, cold, and hungry. So, I decided to go down with the
dog right away. But first I gave it to a whole bunch of hugs and
kisses and some water and some food. And then we started
heading down.

When we were about two-thirds of the way back down to the trail-head and were coming around a corner guess who's coming up the trail? My friend the owner of the dog! There's no one but me, and the dog on the mountain and the dog's owner shows up! I say to my friend *"What the heck are you doing here?"* and followed quickly by *"Guess what? I found Missy!"*

And he tells me that he had no plans of coming up and looking for the dog but the idea and the powerful urge spontaneously came over him a few hours earlier and while he was in the middle of a class at university, so he hightailed it up. And guess what time it was when he got the urge to come to Blackmore Peak? Exactly the same time that I made my decision to go up the Blackmore Peak trail!

As soon as the universe knew that I was actually going to go up the trail and intersect with the dog it notified my friend to come up and join us! Does everyone reading this see the profound significance of this? My prayer was answered, and the people who dearly loved the dog were guided to the reunion and final rescue of the dog! Even though neither of us was planning to do it. I just set the intention and sent the prayer into the universe, and the universe guided us to the outcome we desired!

It's kind of like a love triangle. All three back together again! That is the power of prayer which is the power of intention and any intention motivated by love is a super powerful intention, and magic can happen!

Chapter 22

The Hidden Insidious Effects of Trapped Negative Emotions

The subject of Trapped Emotions is one that many are not aware of, especially if they're not familiar with energy and the energy body. A more common term for Trapped Emotions is "emotional baggage." Although most people probably think that emotional baggage is just memories of emotionally traumatic life experiences, it is much more than that and has a slew of detrimental effects that most are unaware of.

Just about everyone has some emotional baggage from painful life experiences. But it's not all in your head like most people assume. Our emotional baggage is very real, and unbeknownst to most of us, it is causing profound negative effects on the quality of our lives including our health, relationships, happiness, success, and much more — including whether we'll be able to continue participating in the ongoing Ascension process!

Trapped negative emotions are one of the big hidden reasons why so many people are unwittingly manifesting needless adversity in their lives and sabotaging the manifestation of their true desires.

Despite the adverse effects of the trapped emotions that virtually all of us hold, the good news is that our trapped emotions can be released and by doing so many undesirable manifestations will often disappear from our lives. And perhaps more importantly, by learning some new skills, adopting some new perspectives about the challenges and people in our lives, and changing ourselves (our state of being) we can avoid creating new trapped emotions, and their harmful effects, in the future.

The Detrimental Effects of Trapped Emotions

Trapped negative emotions are the root cause of, or a significant contributing factor in, almost everything that goes wrong with your physical body. Including dysfunction, disease, and pain. They also contribute to creating dysfunction in your relationships, career, and in many other areas of your life.

And trapped negative emotions often contribute to maintaining the undesirable circumstances that spawned them in the first place. And worse yet, they can even attract (via the Law of Attraction) similar adversity in the future. Trapped emotions are a potent force that is ever present and silently blocking you from manifesting health, happiness, and success.

And last but not least, if we don't clear our trapped negative emotions, we will not be able to continue to participate in the ongoing ascension that is taking place here on Earth. If you are unaware of this, there is something profound underway on our planet. The long heralded great spiritual transformation of Humanity is underway. The energetic frequency of everything on Earth is rising, including the frequency of our bodies and consciousness. More and more people all over the planet are awakening and remembering their higher selves and the greater reality. More and more people's level of consciousness is shifting upwards as well. This shift in consciousness will ultimately (over the next 20 to 80 years or so) completely transform ourselves and our world.

One of the things that can hold us back from this process is our trapped negative emotions. They are literally like an anchor that will hold us down, not allowing us to ascend with everyone else if we don't clear them from our bodies. As the frequency of everything rises the detrimental effects of having trapped emotions will be amplified and those holding them will experience increasing health issues and adversity. So more than ever, it is extremely important to clear one's emotional baggage.

With all the detrimental effects that Trapped Emotions cause I think you can appreciate why releasing them could be very helpful. Before we get into that let's explore what Trapped Emotions really are and how they form in a bit more detail.

What Are Trapped Emotions and How Do They Form

Emotional baggage isn't just memories trapped in your head it's also negative energy that is trapped in various other parts of your body. Everything is energy — matter is energy, thoughts are energy, emotions are energy, and of course, your physical body is energy. Your body is a very complex set of energy patterns (energy of a very slow vibration that is visible and seems solid) and the energy of negative emotions interferes with the energy that composes your body and its functions. That's why it causes pain, dysfunction, and disease. Besides the effects trapped negative emotions have on your health they also are a potent force that, by the Law of Attraction, attract undesirable circumstances into your life.

Far too often many of us suppress and hold on to the negative emotions associated with unpleasant life experiences — emotions like anger, resentment, frustration, fear, sorrow, grief, despair, shame, unworthiness and so many more. When we do this, we trap the negative energy of the emotions in the energy field of our bodies.

Why do we suppress the negative emotions that we feel from painful life experiences? We suppress them because we don't like feeling that way and we just want it to stop, we just want to get rid of them. What we don't realize is that by forcing ourselves to stop feeling the uncomfortable feelings we aren't getting rid of them we're just hiding them from ourselves. The energy of unfelt (unreleased) emotions just stays in our body's energy field, where they arose in the first place. This is why we say the emotion is trapped — we didn't want to fully feel those feelings and hence release them, so they stay in the energy field of our body.

Emotionally Charged Memories

Your trapped emotions aren't just isolated clumps of negative energy, they are associated with the memories of the experiences that "caused" them. As an aside, memories are energy patterns too, just like everything else.

Our memories of our traumatic experiences often have very strong negative emotional energy associated with them — that is, some memories are highly charged. And those charges stay there until you release them, but you don't because you don't like thinking about that experience and feeling the way it makes you feel. Or if you do revisit those memories, and you feel the feelings, you hold onto the feelings because you want to — for instance, you want to remain angry and resentful about the perceived harm another "did" to you.

But ultimately, your perception of any event, and the emotions that you feel because of it, is your choice despite how it seems. The choice to play the victim arises from not wanting to take full responsibility for all your experiences and how you interpret them. More about this important topic later in this article.

The emotional charges associated with your memories can vary widely — from highly negative, to neutral or none, to highly positive. But of course, positively charged memories are not a problem, it's the negatively charged ones that cause all the problems.

And it's not the memories themselves that are the problem. You can't avoid your experiences being recorded as memories. There's nothing wrong with memories, they are just objective recordings of what happened. It's your interpretation of those experiences that creates the emotional charge associated with the memories.

The reason you store the emotional charges with your memories is because during and after the experience that triggered them, while you were intellectually and emotionally processing the experience, you didn't fully express, and hence release, the emotions associated with the experience. They were uncomfortable, and you didn't want to keep feeling them. You may have also judged the emotions you were having as being "wrong" or "bad" — believing that you are not supposed to feel that way (for instance, some believe it's wrong to be angry) making you feel even more uncomfortable with having those emotions.

One of the keys to avoid trapping emotions is to understand that there's nothing wrong with feeling any type of emotion, including uncomfortable ones. If we stop identifying with and judging our emotions and instead see them as natural and allow ourselves to feel them completely and let them flow out of us, and hence be released, we'll be much better off.

Instead, we bury them with the memory rather than fully feeling them at the moment and then releasing them. We force ourselves to stop feeling them and they get trapped in there with the memory. We think we've deleted the memory and associated feelings but all we've done is hidden them from ourselves — suppressed them and they become effectively trapped within us.

And each time we revisit those memories and dredge up the associated emotions we just reinforce the memories and their associated emotional charge because we never release them and hence, we unwittingly maintain or even reinforce those trapped emotions and all the undesirable effects they cause.

How Trapped Emotions Affect What You Manifest

Anyone with just a superficial understanding of the Law of Attraction understands the importance of deliberately choosing their thoughts and keeping them as positive and optimistic as possible. But what about your subconscious thoughts? Your subconscious mind has a big effect on what you manifest in your life.

The detrimental effects of emotionally charged memories (trapped emotions) arise largely because they subconsciously affect how we think, feel, and behave and hence adversely affect what we experience and create. You may be trying your best to think positively at the conscious level, while subconsciously you are having lots of negative thoughts and feelings that are contradicting your conscious thoughts. The more trapped emotions you have, the more subconscious negative thoughts and feelings you have that are silently eroding or negating your conscious point of attraction and blocking the manifestation of your true desires and attracting adversity.

Also, we sometimes revisit those emotionally charged memories on a more conscious level — often more frequently than we are aware of — just to wallow in anger, blame, self-pity, etc. or when we're worrying that something similar might occur in the future.

When you revisit your emotionally charged memories it's like you're reexperiencing the event with all of its thoughts and feelings. Which is the perfect formula for manifesting more of the same. It's like the practice of intentionally visualizing and imagining your desires to hasten their manifestation except in this case your just remembering a past experience but the effect is the same — you are attractIng it!

When you revisit your traumatic memories and reexperience the emotions you are creating a very potent point of attraction which is increasing the chances of experiencing more of the same. And most of us are revisiting our traumatic memories and feelings far more often than we're aware of. It's kind of just a bad habit.

This is probably why the Buddha shared these words of wisdom with the world:

> *Do not dwell in the past, do not worry about the future, concentrate the mind on the present moment.*

Releasing Your Trapped Emotions

So, I hope I've impressed on you the profound detrimental effects that your trapped emotions are having on the quality of your life. The good news is there are many ways you can release or clear your trapped emotions and gain relief from their adverse effects.

There are many different methods ranging from what I call passive external methods to active internal methods. What differentiates passive external methods from active internal methods is the degree which they require you to identify your trapped emotions and the experiences that created them, and to understand why you chose to interpret and respond to those experiences in the way you did, and perhaps prompts you to learn new ways of responding.

Because completely passive external methods of releasing trapped emotions do not require you to identify or understand the trapped emotions and their genesis, they are quick and easy as compared to methods that lie on the active internal end of the scale. But their downside is you don't learn anything that will help you avoid responding differently to situations in the future and hence avoid trapping more emotions.

In the following sections I'm going to explore some of the more well-known methods of releasing trapped emotions. There are probably more that I am not aware of and many variations, but these are a good start at understanding the options. I'm going to start with the methods that are more passive external oriented and then progress to ones that are more active internal.

Sound Therapy

This method has many variations but what they all have in common is the use of sound to affect the energy in your body. One example of this is the use of a series of 6 musical tones called the Solfeggio Frequencies that are said to increasingly raise your vibration when listened to. These tones help dissolve or transmute negative energy such as trapped emotions which effectively releases them from your body and energy system.

This method is a totally passive external method that does not require you to identify your trapped emotions, or the experiences that caused them. Check out this great article about the healing power of the solfeggio frequencies for more info and to listen to the tones.

Third Party Removal

There are a number of energy healers that act as facilitators or intermediaries for non-physical beings who provide the service of removing or dissolving our trapped negative emotional energy. The exact methods used by the various practitioners vary but they all claim to be able to remove your trapped emotions and provide immediate long-lasting relief from their adverse effects.

This is a completely passive external method. It does not require you to identify your trapped emotions, or understand what experience was involved in creating them, or change yourself in any way. It simply requires you to want to clear yourself of negative energy and be willing to allow it to occur. A great example of someone who provides this service is Ethan Fox, check out Energy Transfer with Ethan Fox to learn more.

The Emotion Code Method

The Emotion Code method was developed by Dr. Bradley Nelson and it uses muscle testing to quickly and accurately identify what trapped emotions a person has and what experience created them.

Muscle testing is a procedure that accesses the subconscious mind (and infinite intelligence) to get yes or no and true or false answers to specific questions regarding what trapped emotions we have and their cause. Apparently, the spirit realms have provided us this query tool to facilitate clearing our negative trapped emotions which is essential if we are to awaken and ascend according to the divine plan because trapped negative emotions are one of the key things that are stopping us from achieving this.

Once one has identified a trapped emotion, they then state their intention to release the emotion and swipe a magnet (which produces an electromagnetic energy field) over the governing energy meridian of their body to amplify their intention and to release the emotion.

The Emotion Code method is a hybrid method that lies somewhere between passive external and active internal. Even though the direct method is fairly passive and external in and of itself. Dr. Nelson, in his book The Emotion Code does address the changes of attitude and perspective that can greatly help in releasing old emotional wounds and avoid creating new ones.

Overall, I think this is one of the best methods and one that anyone can learn and administer to oneself or one's friends and family. Dr. Nelson provides a thorough explanation of the whole topic and teaches the methodology in his book The Emotion Code which I highly recommend.

Regression Therapy

Regression Therapy uses hypnosis to access a person's subconscious mind to find forgotten and repressed experiences and the trapped negative emotions associated with them. The process facilitates the release of those trapped negative emotions and it also encourages the subject to change the way they interpreted those experiences and to change themselves so they will respond differently in the future making it perhaps the most active internal method available.

Other Methods

There are a bunch of other methods that claim to release trapped emotions that may or may not be effective. Here are a few of them: The Sedona Method, Access Bars, and Emotional Freedom Technique (EFT / Tapping) — there are certainly others.

Shortcomings of These Methods

The problem with many of these methods is that even though they can clear your accumulated trapped negative emotions and the undesirable manifestations they cause from your life they do not ensure that you won't trap more emotions in the future. And this is because they do not require you to change yourself — the way you interpret and respond to life's traumatic experiences.

No Longer Creating Trapped Emotions

So how do you ensure you don't trap more negative emotions in the future? By understanding how your current state of being is contributing to how you interpret and respond to challenging situations and learning a new way of being that responds differently. After all it is how you interpreted and responded to your past experiences that made them "traumatic" and "emotionally charged" and caused you to trap negative emotions in the first place.

The Greek Stoic philosopher, Epictetus, had this to say about the importance of how you respond to life's challenges:

*It's not what happens to you, but how you react
to it that matters.*

Here are several changes you can make to yourself that can
change how you interpret and respond to life's challenging
situations. Making these changes will not only improve how you
feel as these situations are occurring but will also greatly reduce
the chances of trapping emotions.

Here they are:

- Learn to deliberately choose your emotions rather
  than being emotionally reactive.
- Allow yourself to fully feel whatever emotions arise
  without judgment.
- Become more forgiving and less judgmental.
- Take full responsibility for everything you experience.
- Look for the pearl of wisdom in every situation and
  learn the lesson rather than blaming.

Let's explore each of these in more depth.

Reducing Your Emotional Reactivity

One of the things that contributes to the creation of trapped
negative emotions is your level of emotional reactivity.
Emotional reactivity is when you unconsciously react to

situations with strong negative emotions. It's when you let circumstances dictate how you feel and respond rather than deliberately choosing how you want to feel and respond. It's your knee jerk reactions that you have to life's happenings.

One thing that can help you transcend reactivity is being aware that **you, and only you, choose your emotions**. Many people believe that their emotions are caused by what someone else is doing or the situation they find themselves in. You've seen this belief in action if you've heard people saying things like *"My husband makes me so mad... or That made me so depressed... or That put me in such a bad mood."*

Of course, this is kind of ridiculous because no one but you chooses how to interpret and respond to situations — no one can make you feel any emotion that you don't choose to feel. Things that happen to you do not determine the emotions that you feel. Although you may not have deliberately chosen every circumstance you find yourself in, you do have the ability to choose how you think, feel, and act. No matter what happens, you ultimately are responsible for how you respond.

Many of us unwittingly fall victim to our emotions at times. Our knee-jerk emotional reactions can happen so fast that it seems like there isn't any time to choose differently. If you are late for an appointment, you may automatically feel anxious. If someone treats you rudely, you might automatically feel offended. When you are insulted or abused, you may immediately feel resentful or angry in response.

All of us experience disturbing situations occasionally but unless you take responsibility for how you respond, you will simply react. When you allow yourself to react, your subconscious mind and your ego often will deliver negative emotion, likely ones used in similar circumstances in the past. This is because you are allowing the situation to trigger your automatic response patterns, but you don't have to. You can override them and deliberately choose how to respond. In every new situation you encounter you can choose to feel and respond differently than you have in the past.

You always are choosing your emotions it is just that you are either doing it unconsciously or consciously. Simply becoming aware of this can greatly facilitate you becoming less emotionally reactive. Of course, setting an intention to become more deliberate about how you respond to life's bumps can help greatly also. It's not always easy but you can get better at it with intent and practice.

So, here's a practical suggestion on how to avoid simply reacting unconsciously the next time you are faced with a challenging situation. When you feel that surge of negative emotions starting to build (and with practice noticing this will become easier) take a short pause and breathe. This gives yourself the space to connect with your higher-self and remember who you really are or want to be and to consider what response will be the most productive, loving, and compassionate. And only then respond in a deliberate fashion based on that.

Of course, one of the keys to consistently choosing to feel and respond differently is to fundamentally change how you interpret situations. And the key to this is to adopt new beliefs and attitudes about people and situations. What I'm talking about here is adopting a more understanding, forgiving, less judgmental attitude, taking more responsibility for your experiences (rather than the tendency to blame others), and focusing on the pearl of wisdom that these situations almost always contain, rather than focusing on the problem itself. I will explore all of these in some detail shortly but first let's take a look at how to handle the emotions that do arise, so you can reduce the chances that you will repress them and trap them.

Allowing Yourself to Feel the Emotions Fully

Regardless of what emotions do arise you must not judge those emotions or yourself for having them. Doing this is part of the reason that you suppress and trap them.

To ensure that you don't trap them you must allow yourself to feel those emotions fully — without judgment. There's nothing wrong with how you feel, they are just feelings. Let them flow through you and feel them completely. Really let yourself vent

— jump up and down, scream, cry, or whatever you need to do and just keep doing it until the feeling dissipates.

You might want to remove yourself from the situation before you do this but let yourself do this. And like I said, and this is very important, don't judge what you are feeling or yourself for feeling that way — this will only encourage you to suppress those emotions, which is what we are trying to avoid.

The goal is to feel your feelings fully and then let them go. If you hold a grudge or can't stop thinking about a situation it's probably because you haven't released the emotional charge that you allowed that situation to create within you.

Becoming More Forgiving and Less Judgmental

One of the ways that you can change how you interpret and hence respond to events is nurture a less judgmental and more forgiving attitude. The inability to let go and forgive is one of the primary reasons why people end up with trapped negative emotions. Understanding the reasons why you are less forgiving and non-judgmental than perhaps you could be, and how to change that is therefore an important step on the road to no longer creating trapped emotions. Let's take a look at some of them.

Reducing Your Egoic Pride

One of the reasons that people find it difficult to let go and forgive is egoic pride. Although there are positive types of pride, egoic pride is an insidious and damaging type of pride that ultimately ends up harming those that wield it even though they are likely completely unaware of this fact. And sadly, it is very common.

Egoic pride expresses as selfishness, jealousy, hatred, resentment, superiority, ill will, or anger toward others. Egoic pride leads those that are in its grip down a dark path to strong negative emotional reactivity, often starting with the feeling of resentment. And of course, this makes them unwilling to forgive others. Instead, they hold on to the real or imagined wrongs they have suffered, and allow themselves to feel angry, frustrated, resentful, etc. And in the worst case it may even drive them to pursue retribution against those they perceive have hurt them.

What they unfortunately don't realize is how damaging holding onto negative emotions is to themselves — because if they did, they would certainly choose to change their ways.

Becoming aware of the nature and consequences of egoic pride and to what degree we are in its grip can be very helpful in nurturing the ability to be less reactive, more forgiving, and to let go. The problem is that even though it's very easy to recognize egoic pride in others, it is often very difficult to recognize in ourselves. But of course, with increased self-awareness you should be able to catch it in yourself. A sure sign that your egoic pride might be out of control is if you are easily and quickly offended (and brought to anger, frustration, and resentment) and tend to hold a grudge.

You will not be punished for your anger, you will be punished by your anger.

— Buddha

The Liberating Effect of Forgiveness

It is so important to understand how much that letting go of old hurt feelings helps you. You may think that you are justified in holding on to hurt feelings because it punishes those that hurt you. But in truth, holding on to negative emotions hurts only you, not them. Those that you perceive have wronged you may or may not be aware of how you feel and may or may not suffer along with you. But your choice to hold onto the perceived wrong ultimately hurts you far more than anyone else.

The Buddha eloquently echoed this point when he uttered these words of wisdom:

*Holding on to anger is like grasping a hot coal
with the intent of throwing it at someone else;
you are the one who gets burned.*

They may have done something truly horrible and it may seem impossible to let it go. This is your opportunity to do something truly liberating — you can choose to forgive them unconditionally and free yourself of all of the negativity associated with the situation.

Forgiveness and Unconditional Love

One of the keys to becoming more forgiving is to foster the quality of unconditional love and compassion within ourselves. These qualities will motivate us to look beyond the surface of another's actions to try to understand why they behaved that way. These qualities will enhance your ability to understand how and why they feel the way the do and why they have behaved the way they did.

When our hearts are full of love and compassion, we are much more likely to get beyond our own self-centeredness, and we are much more forgiving, patient, and kind, we are much more interested in the welfare of others and making others happy, and we are much less likely to develop trapped emotions. Our tendency will be to overlook the faults and weaknesses of others, rather than to judge them. Our tendency will be to look deeper into the reasons behind another's actions and feelings and understand that they are just doing the best they can based on the sum of all their experiences up to this point in their life.

Beyond Forgiveness

We may even realize the deep wisdom that if we were in their shoes, truly in their shoes, we would feel and do the same. And so often the harm we do to each other is unintentional or happens out of ignorance and looking beyond the surface will often make us realize this. These realizations take you to the lofty understanding that everyone is doing the best they can given their life history and experiences up to this point and that it really could not be any other way. Then you begin to see the challenges as simply opportunities for everyone to learn and grow.

The qualities of unconditional love and compassion are worth nurturing within yourself because they will create a life of positivity that will have you floating joyously high above the negativity and drama of most of the everyday world.

Taking Full Responsibility for Your Experiences

A very important realization that is both critical to self-empowerment and greatly facilitates changing how you interpret and respond to life's challenges is taking full responsibility for everything that comes into your experience.

For anyone on the road to self-mastery and mastery of their creatorship a crucial understanding is that blaming others is a hugely disempowering habit. When you blame others you implicitly are saying to yourself and the Universe "something outside of myself, over which I have no control, is the cause of my experiences and my happiness."

Which of course is not true, because you are creating your reality absolutely without exception with your very own thoughts and beliefs regardless of whether you understand how. And by not embracing this you effectively abdicate your creatorship and you unconsciously create your experience which will likely contain more adversity and undesirable things than you would prefer.

The most productive attitude is "there is nothing being done to me." By the Law of Attraction, you draw to yourself every experience your soul requires, in order to learn, evolve and grow.

Life isn't happening to you, it's happening because of you and for you.

When you accept this completely, you will begin to really see the gift in every situation, however challenging, and you will extract the pearl of wisdom from it and use it to propel your growth and evolution, and you will never again dwell on your past experiences with the slightest amount of resentment or remorse.

Focusing on the Pearl of Wisdom

Another way that you can change how you interpret and respond to life's challenging situations is to always focus on the pearl of wisdom that every challenging situation almost always provides you — rather than focusing on the immediate problem or offense.

Is there a higher principle or ideal that can be gleaned from the situation? Is there a lesson to be learned? What pearl of wisdom does the situation contain that can help you grow to be a wiser, more loving, and happier being?

Focusing on the wisdom to be gleaned from, and the growth opportunity provided by, every situation takes you to a higher plane far above judgment, blame, recrimination, and any other negativity to something far more productive. And it will greatly increase your chances of never trapping negative emotions again and unwittingly suffering their insidious damaging consequences.

Cultivating Self-Awareness

One of the key skills that is important to transforming yourself so you can forever become free of negativity and the threat of trapping negative emotions is self-awareness. Self-awareness is essential to all forms of healing and change. Without awareness of your state of being no change is possible — awareness enables the choice to make a change. While this may seem obvious it is often overlooked. Without becoming aware of our defensive and negative thoughts and judgments how are we to choose to be different.

Nurturing and cultivating greater self-awareness is crucial to all growth including growing beyond emotional reactivity and holding on to negative emotions. One thing you can do that will help with this is to set the intention to become more aware of mental and emotional habits and behaviors. You might perhaps even ask for help and guidance — from the Universe, or God, or your spirit guides, or your higher-self, whatever works for you.

And believe it or not this will actually help you begin to catch yourself reacting in ways that perhaps you'd like to change. When you do catch yourself reacting go ahead and acknowledge it and give thanks that it has come to your attention. For example, you might say to yourself, *"I'm feeling irritable for some reason. I'm really glad I can see that."* The increased awareness that you will cultivate will give you the opportunity to learn, grow, and change.

If you always respond to becoming aware of your thoughts and feelings with something like *"I'm really glad I can see that"* and you feel genuinely pleased and grateful to be able to notice them and have the opportunity to address the source of them then you will find yourself quickly becoming more and more self-aware. And as you do you will find yourself gaining deeper and deeper insights into yourself and making more and more healthy changes. Just remember to be non-judgmental about anything you find in yourself that you would prefer to change. You don't have to make yourself wrong to change yourself, in fact, it makes it harder. It is always most productive to notice your thoughts, feelings, and behaviors lovingly and without judgment.

With sincere intention and practice you can become very self-aware and this will facilitate much learning, growth, and change in yourself for the better.

Summing it Up

Trapped negative emotions are one of the biggest causes of all sorts of adverse effects on your health and what you can manifest in your life. You create them when you interpret and respond to situations that unfold in your life with strong negative emotions that you are uncomfortable with completely feeling so you suppress them, which only traps them in the energy field of your body and hides them from you.

There are quite a few ways that you can release or clear existing trapped emotions from yourself that will give you relief from there adverse effects. But ultimately, you will need to fundamentally change yourself if you want to avoid creating new trap emotions and subjecting yourself to their adverse effects in the future.

The choice to clear your trapped emotions and learn how to avoid creating more in the future should be a no-brainer once you understand how damaging they are to the quality of your life.

To your success!

About the Author

J eff is an avid student and teacher of spiritual metaphysics. In the spring of 2014, after spending his entire life as an

atheist/agnostic and scientific materialist, he experienced a profound "awakening".

He experienced enhanced intuition, constant synchronicities, a heightened sense of the beauty of everything around him, and intense fascination with many topics that he had heretofore ignored, and frequent moments of utter bliss where he would break down and cry like a baby, and lots and lots of good luck.

After three or four months of constant magic that he couldn't explain in any rational or scientific way, he finally threw his hands up in the air, surrendered to the Universe as he uttered these words in his mind — *"OK, OK, I give up. The Universe isn't what I thought, not with all this divine magic going on. I'll bet it has something to do with spirituality, and I intend to get to the bottom of it!"*

This set him on a "quest for the truth and he dove headlong and wholeheartedly into a study of spirituality and metaphysics. It wasn't long before he had a completely new understanding of himself and the nature of reality that resonated deeply with him and that he wanted to share with the world. So, he created his website, *Divine Cosmos*, and his YouTube and Facebook channels, and started writing with a passion.

Learn more here:

Jeff's **other books** and **audiobooks**:

http://divine-cosmos.net/books.htm

 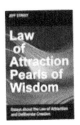 

Website: http://divine-cosmos.net

Facebook: https://www.facebook.com/DivineCosmoz

YouTube: https://www.youtube.com/c/DivineCosmos111

Academy: http://DeliberateCreatorAcademy.com

Made in the USA
Monee, IL
24 May 2021